Salpuri-Chum, A Korean Dance for Expelling Evil Spirits

A Psychoanalytic Interpretation of Its Artistic Characteristics

Eun-Joo Lee and Yong-Shin Kim

Hamilton Books

An Imprint of
Rowman & Littlefield
Lanham • Boulder • New York • Toronto • Plymouth, UK

Copyright © 2017 by Hamilton Books
4501 Forbes Boulevard, Suite 200, Lanham, Maryland 20706
Hamilton Books Acquisitions Department (301) 459-3366

Unit A, Whitacre Mews, 26-34 Stannary Street,
London SE11 4AB, United Kingdom

All rights reserved
Printed in the United States of America
British Library Cataloguing in Publication Information Available

Library of Congress Control Number: 2016962543
ISBN: 978-0-7618-6887-3 (pbk : alk. paper)—ISBN: 978-0-7618-6888-0 (electronic)

∞™ The paper used in this publication meets the minimum requirements of American National Standard for Information Sciences Permanence of Paper for Printed Library Materials, ANSI/NISO Z39.48-1992.

Contents

Preface		v
1	Psychoanalysis and Art	1
	Limits of Human Being and the Ego Ideal	1
	The Task and Form of Art	4
	Notes	9
2	Meaning of the Word Salpuri and the Emotional Dynamics of the Korean People	11
	The Meaning of the Word Salpuri	11
	Theory of the Collective Unconscious	14
	Emotional Dynamics of the Korean People	18
	Notes	22
3	Shamanic Ritual as a Way to Expel Evil Spirits	25
	The Korean People's Traditional Perception of Death	25
	Gut as Shamanic Ritual for Salpuri	28
	Sinawi Rhythm as the Musical Accompaniment of Gut	33
	Notes	37
4	The Development of Salpuri-Chum	39
	Gwangdae-Chum and Gisang-Chum	39
	The Role of Han Sung-Jun for Modern Salpuri-Chum	43
	Basic Structure of Salpuri-Chum and Its Meaning	45
	Notes	46
5	Three Main Styles of Salpuri-Chum	49
	Han Young-Sook Style	49
	Lee Mae-Bang Style	50
	Kim Sook-Ja Style	52

	Notes	53
6	Other Styles of Salpuri-Chum as Local Cultural Treasures	55
	Kwon Myung-Hwa Style	55
	Choi Sun Style	56
	Kim Bok-Ryun Style	58
	Kim Ran Style	59
	Lee Eun-Joo Style	60
	Notes	62
7	Salpuri-Chum and Other Korean Traditional Dances	63
	Other Korean Traditional Dances as National Cultural Treasures	63
	Salpuri-Chum Distinguished from Other Dances and Its Current Situation	68
	Notes	71
8	Aesthetics of Salpuri-Chum	73
	Philosophy and Artistic Form of Salpuri-Chum	73
	The Beauty of Salpuri-Chum	77

Bibliography	81
Korean Publications	81
English Publications	83
Sources of Photographs	87
Index	89
About the Authors	93
Lee Eun-Joo (李銀珠; Pen name, Noeul: 露乙)	93
Kim Yong-Shin (金容新; Pen name, Yidang: 怡堂)	94

Preface

We have been discussing the Korean traditional dance known as Salpuri-Chum for a long time. The main focuses of these discussions were the philosophical and psychoanalytic meanings, and the artistic beauties, of this dance. In this time, we discovered some new elements which we had not seriously considered thus far in understanding this dance. These elements were very helpful in illustrating, in more detail, the main characteristics of Salpuri-Chum.

There are several Korean traditional dances which have been selected as intangible national cultural treasures in Korea. All of them have not only their own history and philosophical background but also the attractive artistic beauties. Among these dances, Salpuri-Chum is unique. Unlike other traditional dances, this dance originated from the Korean shamanic ritual which was named *Gut*. Gut is performed even in the present Korean society.

Of course, the names and the procedures of Gut are a little different according to the different regions. But its essential meaning is same, which is to pray to a god for our well-being, and to expel evil spirits which may harm living persons. In order to fulfill the purpose of Gut, a shaman utters an incantation and moves her or his body; and several traditional musicians play a very interesting rhythm following the shaman's movements. This is called Sinawi rhythm.

Sinawi music does not have detailed sheet music, and its rhythm does not follow a regular determined beat. Thus, it is very improvisatorial. In general, the dancer dances according to the musical accompaniment. However, in Gut the musical accompaniment is played according to the shaman's movements. Salpuri-Chum follows this tradition of Gut in its performance. This is the main reason why this dance is different from other Korean traditional dances.

From this view, we finally decided to introduce this dance to the western society where English is widely used as a common language. Cultures cannot be understood as simply good or bad. The different cultures are, in fact, a master key to understanding human life. It is very meaningful to understand other cultures, because this understanding helps to destroy the barriers that separate us from others.

On this assumption, we began to write this book. Lee, as a dance artist, explains the legacy of Korean shamanic dance, and the process by which Salpuri-Chum developed into a modern theatrical dance. She also illustrates the artistic meaning of Salpuri-Chum by discussing the structure and movements of the dance, as well as the main characteristics of Sinawi music. Kim, as a psychoanalytic social theorist, layers his psychoanalytic interpretations into the explanation. In doing so, he will discuss the essential elements of the Korean people's emotional dynamics.

Indeed, the main task of psychoanalysis can be seen as the same as that of art, because the main subject of both areas is emotion. The artists try to symbolize our emotion, and the psychoanalytic social theorists try to illustrate our emotional dynamics reflected in culture. Therefore, a psychoanalytic social theorist and a dance artist can be complementary partners in the study of Salpuri-Chum. Through this study, as co-authors, we try to illustrate the artistic characteristics of Salpuri-Chum as a representation of the Korean people's unconscious.

In this study, we will first discuss not only our desire to solve our problems derived from the limits of the human being and the civilization, but also the artistic form related to the desire. This aims at illustrating the main characteristic of art as a reflection of our ego ideal. In addition, we will discuss the meaning of Salpuri as reflecting the Korean people's collective unconscious. In this process, we will explain the Korean people's emotional dynamics. After these discussions, we will illustrate the main characteristics of Gut, as a shamanic ritual, and Sinawi rhythm, as the musical accompaniment of the ritual.

In the main discourse, we will trace the developmental history of Salpuri-Chum. As we proceed, we will note the influences of the traditional dances, such as *Gwangdae-Chum* (a dance of traditional players) and *Gisang-Chum* (a dance of traditional female entertainers), on Salpuri-Chum. Also, we will introduce Han Sung-Jun, the pioneer who created Salpuri-Chum as a theatrical modern dance. Then we will explain the three main styles of Salpuri-Chum, and the other styles as intangible local cultural treasures.

Finally, we will show the differences between Salpuri-Chum and other Korean traditional dances, as intangible national cultural treasures. We will discuss the current situation of Salpuri-Chum, in which there is no successor to the title of living human cultural treasure in this field. Then we will summarize the philosophy and artistic form of Salpuri-Chum, and the beauties of Salpuri-Chum.

Salpuri-Chum reflects not only the Korean people's belief system about destiny, but also their desire to change their destiny by resolving their misfortunes. Therefore, Salpuri-Chum is an artistic performance for resolving the Korean people's *Hahn* (a very complicated concept as a kind of lamentation including wish). In this case, it is a form of sublimation. Moreover, Salpuri-Chum can be seen as an effort to change the pain of reality into beauty on the basis of the Korean People's *Heung* (merriment). This is a form of "immanence."

In addition, one of the special characteristics of Salpuri-Chum is improvisation based on Sinawi rhythm, where the dancer can be a conductor. The improvisational character also reflects the Korean people's unconscious. Furthermore, Salpuri-Chum is unique in its use of a piece of white fabric. The fabric, as a symbol of the Korean people's ego ideal, signifies Salpuri-Chum's focus as a dance for resolving their Hahn. The fabric is also a tool for the creation of beautiful shapes. These shapes, by harmonizing with a dancer's movements, create various artistic scenes.

Eun-Joo Lee and Yong-Shin Kim

Chapter One

Psychoanalysis and Art

LIMITS OF HUMAN BEING AND THE EGO IDEAL

Human beings are not self-satisfied.[1] First, we are embodied, eternal spirits held in mortal flesh, so we strain against limits. We want to live forever, yet we have to die. All living beings have to die—therefore, to live means to die. Of course, we can pass on our DNA to our descendants, but this cannot fulfill our wish to live forever. This makes us unhappy.

Second, we are divided sexually into male and female, so we yearn for unity. This means that we are not sexually self-satisfied. In certain circumstances, some fishes can change their sex. We can change our sex through medical surgery; however, we cannot beget children in this case. Of course, we can partly feel a certain sexual pleasure through masturbation. But this also cannot fulfill our wish to transmit our DNA to our descendants through sexual union.

Third, we are individuals living in a society, so we experience disharmony. Many people have argued that we are social beings. Even so, there has been no perfect harmony between individuality and society. Throughout history, many philosophers have tried to find a way to harmonize between them; however, there is not yet a theory which satisfies our wish. There always have been conflicts between the values of society and that of individuality. This may be derived from our instinct for self-realization.

The disharmony between individuality and society can also be explained in terms of our discontent in civilization. This is closely related to the conflicts between individuality and society. In this view, we can easily see that civilization makes us unhappy even as it partly protects us from violent death. Hobbes argues that in the state of nature everyone strives against everyone, meaning the most important desire is self-preservation to avoid violent death; therefore, we created civilization in the hopes of preserving ourselves.[2] But the civilization we created still does not make us happy, because it represses our desires for self-realization. This means that self-preservation is not a necessary and sufficient condition for our happiness.

Nietzsche emphasizes self-realization, as such, as another important element for our happiness.[3] In this sense, Freud discusses two sides of civilization, protection and repression, in his noted work, *Civilization and Its Discontents*. We can protect our bodies in civilization, yet, for that protection, we must repress our desires in the name of civilized values. This is the contradiction, and the inherent discontent of civilization.

Despite the discontents of civilization and its limiting of self-satisfaction, we continually yearn for fulfillment—the desire to return to the womb, in Freudian psychoanalysis. Freud, in "On Narcissism," argues as follows:

> He [man] is not willing to forgo his narcissistic perfection in his childhood; and if, as he develops, he is disturbed by the admonition of others, and his own critical judgment is awakened, he seeks to recover the early perfection, thus wrested from him, in the form of an ego ideal. That which he projects ahead of him as his ideal is merely his substitute for the lost narcissism of his childhood.[4]

This implies that we are removed from the state of narcissistic perfection when we are born, and thus our unhappiness begins. Jay R. Greenberg and Stephen A. Mitchell, in their book *Object Relations in Psychoanalytic Theory*, make the concept of *ego ideal* clear when they explain Freud's "wish model." They hold that Freud, through the wish model, wants to argue that we continually desire to re-establish the original experience of happiness through the ego ideal; it is an instinct for us to seek the pleasure that we once experienced in the womb.[5]

However, we need further explanation of the ego ideal, because Freud sometimes fuses the ego ideal with superego, one of the basic concepts explaining our psychological structure. For instance, in *The Question of Lay Analysis*, Freud writes that "the superego is the vehicle for the phenomenon we call 'conscience.'"[6] Here, Freud understands the superego as a moral code against the ego. But in *The Ego and Id* he states that "The superego, however, is not simply a residue of the earlier object-choices of the id; it also represents an energetic reaction-formation against those choices."[7] This reflects that the superego in its relation to the ego has positive as well as negative perceptions of the child's idealization of his father.

In this sense, Calvin Hall, in *A Primer of Freudian Psychology*, explains the ego ideal as a sub-concept of the superego. According to Hall, the superego has two subsystems, conscience and ego ideal. He points out that "The ego ideal corresponds to the child's conceptions of what his parents consider to be morally good," while the conscience "corresponds to the child's conception of what his parents feel is morally bad."[8]

However, Hall's interpretation has been disputed by some psychoanalysts. For example, Alexander Mitscherlich understands the concept of ego ideal differently from Hall. For him, the ego ideal is not a subsystem of the superego. He argues in *Society without the Father* that the superego "is formed out of the demand of society," while the role of ego ideal "is satisfying the individual's self-respect in a role he has himself chosen within the horizon of his experience."[9] If, like Mitscherlich, we understand the ego ideal as the wish to seek the pleasure experienced in the primary narcissistic perfection, then it is different from the superego.

Chasseguet-Smirgel, a famous theorist in the study of ego ideal, also denies Hall's interpretation. She holds that the ego ideal is the inheritor of primary narcissism, while the superego is the inheritor of the Oedipus complex. She argues, "The superego cuts the child off from his mother," while "the ego ideal pushes the child toward fusion with her."[10] This interpretation implies that the superego is formed from social anxiety, while the ego ideal is formed to solve the anxiety. Therefore, the former tends to promote the recognition of reality, and the latter to restore illusion. In this view, we can say that the superego tends to follow the reality principle, while the ego ideal follows the pleasure principle.

When Freud first focuses on the human being's instincts, he argues that all human beings want to remove pain and obtain pleasure. However, a human being as a social being has to recognize reality for the sake of preservation. This originates from the self-preservative ego instinct. Freud calls it the wish to follow the reality principle.

Through the Oedipal phase, the child begins to learn that he is not a love object of his mother. This realization makes the child unhappy, and in this process the superego is formed. In short, the development of superego continually represses the ego ideal. Despite this, the ego ideal does not give up its desire to follow the pleasure principle. It continually tries to alleviate the pain arising from the activity of the superego, turning to hallucination if necessary.

In addition, the ego ideal as the narcissistic wish cannot be fully controlled by the superego, because the superego is not the fundamental wish to return to the primary narcissistic perfection. Therefore, the desire of ego ideal does not disappear, despite the demand of superego. This resistance means that the superego cannot fully control the ego ideal. Even if the demand of superego is very strong, the ego ideal remains as a latent form. Moreover, it has the power to be reactivated and can absorb the superego in some situations.

If the superego is the wish to follow the reality principle, while the ego ideal is the desire to follow the pleasure principle, the ego ideal cannot be understood as a subsystem of the superego. Rather, it can be seen as a counterpart to the superego. Chasseguet-Smirgel emphasizes that the ego ideal is the desire to achieve full satisfaction, also called the pleasure principle. This pleasure principle competes with the reality principle, which is the superego's desire.[11] All of our activities derive from our basic desire to either find perfection, or overcome our limits and discontents. Therefore, Chasseguet-Smirgel argues that the ego ideal is "a sense of expectation, hope, and promise" of full satisfaction.[12]

From this, we can understand the main reason why we feel some discontents through our limits. If the demand of ego ideal is not present in our minds, we do not feel the pain or discontents derived from our limits. If there is only the reality principle, our limits do not give rise to any discontent. In other words, we can feel the discontents because of the function of ego ideal. Moreover, we continually try to resolve our discontents by the demand of ego ideal. Therefore, we can say that human life is a process of finding satisfaction and healing our wounded minds of the pains derived from our limits. All human activities, then, are based on the demand of ego ideal, which is the wish to realize satisfaction. In this way, the final purpose of philosophy, science, religion, and arts, can also be understood as efforts to overcome our limits and to pacify our discontents.

THE TASK AND FORM OF ART

We can say that the purpose of art is to seek beauty. If so, then what is beauty? It is very difficult to answer this question because the concept of beauty can be understood subjectively. To solve this problem, we need to ask a different type of question: when can we feel beauty, even if the feeling is subjective? The answer to this question can provide us with some clues to understand art.

Among these clues, the most important is that we feel beauty when something moves our emotions. In this sense, many theorists argue that art is to move our emotions. In *Problems of Art*, Susanne Langer argues that art is a symbol of feeling.[13] Nelson Goodman, who devised the term *grue*, also agrees with this interpretation. In *Languages of Art*, he argues that art is an emotional attempt to understand the world.[14] This means that art is not an intellectual attempt.

If art is an emotional attempt to engage with the world, we have to understand the dynamics of our emotions. In seeking to do this, psychoanalysis studying the dynamics of our emotions can provide us with various ideas. Moreover, the main task of psychoanalysis can be seen as the same as that of art. Danielle Knafo argues as follows:

> Both artists and psychoanalysts seek special access to the unconscious, a territory without full and accurate maps, a place where one thing may become another in the wink of an eye, where meaning itself originates not as monolith, but as a deeply layered matrix of possibility, and where every action is multi-determined.[15]

Under this assumption, we can have another question; when are our emotions moved? The answer to this question can be various. However, we can find the essence of the answers by understanding the psychoanalytic theories which we mentioned earlier. According to psychoanalysis, we are satisfied when our emotions are moved. If so, beauty is closely related to this satisfaction because art is an attempt to move our emotions. Moreover, if we are satisfied through the role of ego ideal, we can say that art is a representation of our ego ideal as the wish to return to the primary narcissistic perfection. In this context, we can say that art exists to satisfy ourselves, and also to avoid suffering.

As far as we focus only on the suffering from the limitations of civilization, we, like Herbert Marcuse, can say that reparation or transcendence is the main task of art.[16] In fact, Marcuse emphasizes "the transformation of sexuality into Eros" in his philosophy.[17] However, we need to understand the tasks of art in more detail, as far as art is an attempt to move our emotions. In this regard, Fred Alford, going beyond Marcuse, points out four main tasks of art:

> It helps to make us more at home in the world, it helps us to clarify our emotions, making us more at home with ourselves (this view comes closest to art as reparation); it plays with the world and so creates a realm of personal freedom in an unfree world; and it tell us truth about the world, even when this truth is unpleasant.[18]

Alford's explanation is quite clear, because these four tasks are closely related to our efforts to solve our limits for perfection and to overcome the repression of civilization.

In ancient society, art was entwined with philosophy and religion. It was not a subsystem of philosophy, because art was a means to find truth and perfection, or a means to solve humanity's limits. For the ancient people, the pursuit of beauty was "the key to grasping the basic structure of the world,"[19] because they believed that people could understand the order of the world.

Our ancestors built shrines and idols of their gods, and prayed to the gods in order to solve or overcome the limits of human being. One typical example is a sentence in the Lord's Prayer: "Thy kingdom come. Thy will be done on earth as it is in heaven." (Mt 6:10)[20] In this case, heaven is an ideal situation for perfection, and earth is the reality which represses us.

In praying, people uttered devotions and moved their bodies in rhythm. They also created writings and paintings depicting their moral or spiritual aspirations. All these activities were the means to solve our problems, and those became art when their works moved our emotions. Insofar as their works are focused on the wish to find truth or perfection, it is natural that they move our emotions, which seek perfection through the ego ideal.

In fact, artists' efforts to seek truth or perfection have continued since ancient times. For example, in the eighth century during the kingdom of Silla(新羅: 57 BC–AD 935, a kingdom of the Korean peninsula), a craftsman began to make a bell according to the order of the king. But he failed several times to make a good bell with a wonderful sound. According to the tale, he could produce the bell he wanted only after he had thrown his son into the melting furnace.[21] This story reflects the artist's effort to produce the perfect sound. This bell still exists as the Korea National Treasure, No. 29.

The well-known Korean painting *Mongyoodowondo* (夢遊桃源圖: Paradise in Dream) was created by the renowned artist An Gyun(安堅: ca 1400), in 1447 during the Chosun dynasty (朝鮮: 1392–1910). He reproduced the scene which Anpyungdaegun(安平大君: 1418–1453), a prince of the king Sejong(世宗: 1397–1450), saw in his dream, by imaging the perfect world.[22] He wanted to represent an ideal scene through this work. This is derived from our wish to find a perfect world where we can be satisfied.

We can also find artists' efforts to seek perfection through the spirit of classicism of Europe in the seventeenth and eighteenth centuries. The artists of classicism tried to seek ideal harmony, order, and balance through their works.[23] And even the practice in modern Europe of castration of some male vocalists, in order to maintain their high voices, can also be understood as an effort to seek perfection. The castrated male vocalists, known as *castrato*, contributed to the development of opera in Italy, although they had disappeared after the twentieth century.[24] Many artists have tried to find perfection though their ego ideal even in modern society. In this context, Martin Heidegger explains art as a representation of truth because it seeks to find the hidden truth.[25]

These kinds of efforts can be compared with the effort to find the *Idea* in Plato's philosophy. For Plato, there is a basic *form* that fulfills the perfection of all material beings. This he calls the Idea; therefore, we cannot understand the true forms of matter without finding their Ideas. He argues that the sensible world which we can see is just an image. In his Republic,[26] Plato uses the shadows in the cave to illustrate the meaning of the Ideas. Thus, if people who cannot move are in a cave, and there is a light behind them casting shadows on the wall, they believe that the shadows of things are the true shapes or forms of those things. However, if a man comes out of the cave, he realizes that the things he saw in the cave are not their real forms, but just their images. This means that man can see the true shape of things only under the sunlight; the Idea, therefore, is something like the sunlight.

Apart from a means to seek truth or perfection, art also functions as compensation for the repressed desire in civilization. We are discouraged when what we want is not realized. In this case, we also try to pacify our sorrow derived from the discouragement because our mind automatically wants to keep a stable condition for self-preservation. This is Freud's *constancy principle*, which "is the aim of the psychic apparatus to keep stimulation as close to zero as possible."[27]

Our sorrow may be reduced through religion, which believes in the existence of a god or gods. If a god controls or determines our destiny, we cannot change our fate by ourselves. In this case, our sorrow can be pacified only by a transcendental power. This is a way to find not only the origin of our problems, but also the solution of the problems from the outside, rather than from within our minds. In this way, we sublimate our sorrow through the transcendental power.

We can also find another way to solve our problems, which is to seek other satisfactions to pacify our sorrows. For instance, disappointment in love makes us sorrowful; however, the sorrow may be partly pacified when we realize other desires, because satisfaction in one area may compensate for the sorrow in a different area. We can also refer to this kind of solution as "sublimation." It is related to the psychoanalytical concept of sublimation as a defense mechanism. To the extent we cannot rise above our sorrow in one area, we cannot do anything in other areas. Therefore, we need to sublimate our problems.

As mentioned earlier, Herbert Marcuse advances some very interesting arguments relating to sublimation. For him, the predominance of genital sexuality causes many problems in the libidinal relations of our society. Therefore, he proposes "a transformation of the libido: from sexuality constrained under genital supremacy to erotization of the entire personality" through "reactivation of all erotogenic zones" and "a resurgence of pregenital polymorphous sexuality."[28]

Regarding sublimation, we may ask: can we fully resolve our sorrow through sublimation? It is very difficult to answer this question. However, nobody can deny that the sorrow can be partly pacified by other sources of satisfaction. Therefore, the theory of sublimation is still viable in the understanding of human life.

The repressed desires resulting from civilization make us sorrowful; however, we can partly pacify the sorrow through art. "In civilization, art, unrestricted from the reality, allows us to portray the impossible things. Through art we can conquer Evil and obtain Eternity."[29] By reflecting our dreams, art can appease the repressed desires, at least in part. This can be understood as an effort to sublimate our repressed desires through the imaginable world.

The art based on sublimation or transcendence is the *art of Apollo* in Nietzsche's aesthetics.[30]

There is another way to solve our problem. Psychoanalytically, it is based on the primary narcissism that loves the self when it does not find an external love-object. In his essay *On Narcissism*, Freud maintains that a human being has two sexual objects, an external love-object and one's self, arguing that this primary narcissism is found in everyone.[31] Therefore, we can understand it as an instinct. Fred Alford says that "primary narcissism is not a perversion, of course, but the first stage of psychosexual development, in which the young child's libidinal interests are centered upon himself and his own body."[32]

When our love is rejected by the external love object, we are disappointed. This, of course, makes us unhappy. However, we have some abilities to pacify our sorrow through the constancy principle. One of the abilities is to love our sorrow. As noted above, we can pacify our sorrow through sublimation. However, we cannot sublimate all our problems. If so, we have to solace ourselves by loving the problems. Without this ability, our minds cannot keep a stable condition for self-preservation.

This approach is possible through the primary narcissism. Love of our limits and discontents can be a useful way to pacify our sorrow. Philosophically, the theory of the primary narcissism is closely related to that of *immanence*, a philosophical concept which emphasizes that the cause of a phenomenon is "taking place within the mind of the subject and having no effect outside of it."[33] This theory implies that we can find the solution of our problems in ourselves; thus, this can be understood as the counterpart of the theory of transcendence mentioned above.

In this context, the primary narcissism highlights another aspect of art: the ability to change the pain of reality into something beautiful. This is an effort to love our problems. We see this effort in the realism in the nineteenth century. The artists of realism tried to find beauty in reality; therefore, they rejected idealized images, and drew the real scenes which we can directly see. For instance, Gustave Courbet (1819–1877), a famous French painter, says that we may image the face of an angel through that of our fathers.[34] This implies that we can find the beauty by which our emotions are moved in the reality. The existentialism of the twentieth century also denied idealism, and tried to find beauty in the reality. Thus, the writers of existentialism tried to show that the pain of reality can be also beautiful.

This kind of realism also prevailed in the Korean peninsula at the end of the seventeenth century. After An Gyun, who focused on drawing ideal scenes, Chung Sun(鄭敾: 1676–1759) began drawing real landscapes, which were not the subject of drawings before that time. Kim Hong-Do(金弘道: 1745–?), who succeeded to the spirit of Chung Sun, tried to draw the joys and sorrows of ordinary people. Shin Yoon-Bok(申潤福: 1758–?), going further, drew an erotic scene which was regarded as an impurity in Confucianism, the ruling ideology in that time. *Wolhajeongin*(月下情人: Lovers under Moon), in which a man and a woman enjoy their love under the light of the moon, is a good example of this among his works.

Insofar as we discuss the effort to love our sorrow, we also need to illustrate the meaning of tragedy. In the various tragedies, the heroes or heroines die, which makes us sorrowful. But in spite of their deaths, our emotions can be pacified. Why is this possible? It is because we have the primary narcissistic instinct which loves our sorrow and pain. This is a case in which we can pacify our sorrow by loving our problems. In this situation, we can directly represent our sorrow, and then we may cry. But once we cry, we feel that our sorrow is partly pacified. This process is called *catharsis*. Our sorrow felt in the tragedies can be partly pacified through the catharsis. This can be also one of ways to relieve our problems by solacing ourselves.

According to Nietzsche, the artistic form based on the primary narcissism or immanence is explained as *the art of Dionysus*, which is a counter concept to the art of Apollo.[35] This is a form of immanence. In this sense, we can say all tragedies tend to take this kind of form.

If we agree with Fred Alford's argument about the tasks of art, art has mainly three forms: the art of perfection, the art of sublimation, and the art of immanence. All these form are focused on how we can solve our original limits and discontents in civilization. Of course, all human activities are also originated from the realization of our ego ideal. But, art is different from other activities because it can solve the problems through the imaginary world. In short, art is providing us with very useful ways to solve our problems.

NOTES

1. Yong-Shin Kim, *A Psychoanalytic Interpretation of Art* [in Korean] (Seoul: Nanam, 2008), 34–35; see within English "Summary: A Psychoanalytic Interpretation of Art," 116–17.

2. Laurence Berns, "Thomas Hobbes," *History of Political Philosophy*, ed. Leo Strauss and Joseph Cropsey, 3rd ed. (Chicago: University of Chicago Press, 1987), 402.

3. Huntington Wright, *What Nietzsche Taught* (New York: B.W. Huebsch, 1917), 178.

4. Sigmund Freud, "On Narcissism," in A General Selection from the Works of Sigmund Freud (New York: Doubleday Anchor Books, 1957), 116; also see The Standard Edition of the Complete Psychological Works of Sigmund Freud, trans. and ed. James Strachey, collab. Anna Freud, assist. Alix Strachey and Alan Tyson (hereafter cited as SE), vol. 14, 1914–1916, On the history of the psycho-analytic movement, Papers on metapsychology and Other works (London: The Hogarth Press and the Institute of Psycho-Analysis, 1957), 67–104.

5. Jay R. Greenberg and Stephen A. Mitchell, *Object Relations in Psychoanalytic Theory* (Cambridge: Harvard University Press, 1983), 29.

6. Nandor Fodor and Frank Gaynor, eds., *Freud: Dictionary of Psychoanalysis* (Westport, Conn: Greenwood Press, 1975), s.v. "superego."

7. Sigmund Freud, "The Ego and Id," *SE*, vol. 19, *1923–1925, The Ego and the Id and Other works* (1961), 34.

8. Calvin S. Hall, *A Primer of Freudian Psychology* (New York: World Publishing Company, 1954), 26.

9. Alexander Mitscherlich, *Society without the Father: A Contribution to Social Psychology*, tr. Eric Mosbacher (New York: Harcourt, Brace & World; London: Tavistock Publications, 1969), 127.

10. Janine Chasseguet-Smirgel, "Some Thoughts on the Ego Ideal: A Contribution to the Study of the 'Illness of Ideality,'" *The Psychoanalytic Quarterly* 45 (July 1976): 347.

11. Janine Chasseguet-Smirgel, *The Ego Ideal: A Psychoanalytic Essay on the Malady of the Ideal*, 1st American ed. (New York: W.W. Norton, 1985). In this work, Chasseguet-Smirgel elucidates the function of the ego ideal as a counter desire against the superego. For more detail, see Yong-Shin Kim, *The Ego Ideal, Ideology, and Hallucination* (Lanham, MD: University Press of America, 1992), 43–46.

12. Chasseguet-Smirgel, "Some Thoughts," 350.

13. Susanne Langer, *Problems of Art: Ten Philosophical Lectures* (New York: Scribner's, 1957), quoted in Fred Alford, *Melanie Klein & Critical Social Theory* (New Haven: Yale University Press, 1989), 104.

14. Nelson Goodman, *Languages of Art: An Approach to a Theory of Symbols* (Indianapolis: Bobbs-Merrill, 1968), 242.

15. Danielle Knafo, introduction to *Dancing with the Unconscious: The Art of Psychoanalysis and the Psychoanalysis of Art* (New York: Routledge, 2012).

16. Herbert Marcuse, *The Aesthetic Dimension* (Boston: Beacon Press, 1978), 55–61.

17. Herbert Marcuse, *Eros and Civilization* (Boston: Beacon Press, 1966), 197–221.

18. Alford, *Melanie Klein*, 118.

19. Ibid., 104.

20. *The Holy Bible* (Douay Version), translated from the Latin Vulgate (New York: The Douay Bible House, 1953).

21. Yong-Shin Kim, *Ego Ideal, Ideology, and Hallucination*, 73 (hereafter cited as *EIIH*).

22. *Encyclopedia of Korean Culture*(한국민족문화대백과), s.v. "Mongyoodowondo (몽유도원도)," edited by The Academy of Korean Studies(한국학중앙연구원), accessed October 19, 2016, http://100.daum.net/encyclopedia/view/14XXE0018824. Unfortunately, the original painting is now in the library of Tenri University in Japan.

23. Yong-Shin Kim, *Psychoanalytic Interpretation*, 48.

24. "The Beautiful Gender Castrated(거세당한 아름다운 성)," *SISA Newspeople*, February 26, 2007, http://www.inewspeople.co.kr/news/articleView.html?idxno=1521.

25. Martin Heidegger, "The Origin of the Work of Art," in *Martin Heidegger: Basic Writings*, ed. David Farrell Krell (New York: Harper & Row, 1977), 144–87.

26. Plato, *Great Dialogues of Plato*, Trans. W. H. D. Rouse (New York: A Mentor Book, 1956), 312–41.

27. Greenberg and Mitchell, *Object Relations*, 25.

28. Marcuse, *Eros and Civilization*, 201.

29. Yong-Shin Kim, *Psychoanalytic Interpretation*, 119–20.

30. Ibid., 60.

31. Sigmund Freud, *SE*, 14:88.

32. Fred Alford, *Narcissism: Socrates, the Frankfurt School, and Psychoanalytic Theory* (New Haven: Yale University Press, 1988), 25.

33. *Dictionary.com OnLine*, s.v. "immanence," accessed November 10, 2016, http://www.dictionary.com/browse/immanence.

34. Yong-Shin Kim, *Psychoanalytic Interpretation*, 64.

35. Ibid., 66.

Chapter Two

Meaning of the Word Salpuri and the Emotional Dynamics of the Korean People

THE MEANING OF THE WORD SALPURI

Salpuri is a compound word. It consists of two words, *Sal* and *Puri*. Sal originated from the Chinese letter "煞." In Korea, the letter is pronounced as "Sal" or "Shwae."[1] When we pronounce it as Sal, it means "kill," "totalize," "bind together," "control," "win," and so forth. When we pronounce it as Shwae, it means "very," "fast," and "severe." Pronounced as Sal, a Korean dictionary explains its meaning as "cruel and severe (or harsh) energy which harms the people," "evil spirit," or "harmful ghost."[2] Puri is a pure Korean word. It has also various meanings. In English it implies such words as "solve," "untie" or "unknot," "disentangle," "untwine," "loosen," "unbind," "undo," "unravel," etc.

In discussing Salpuri, Sal as a noun can be generally understood as a "harmful energy," according to the dictionary. However, Sal embodies many implications in Korean culture, especially when we want to illustrate the meaning of Salpuri. Beyond the explanations in the dictionary, it includes the meanings of the following words: "evil spirit," "misfortune," "grudge," "sorrow," or "mourning," and the like.

Therefore, we need to consider another interesting Korean concept, which will help us to understand, in more detail, the meaning of Sal in the word, Salpuri. This concept is *Hahn*. A Korean dictionary simply explains it as a word representing ideas such as "grudge" and "regret" and "lamentation."[3] However, it is rather unusual, and it lacks a direct English equivalent. It, indeed, has various implications when we focus on the unconscious of the Korean people.

There are many studies on Hahn. Among them, Chun Yi-Du, a Korean scholar of literature, provides us with very useful clues to understand the concept of Hahn through his famous book, *A Study on the Structure of Hahn*. He first tries to illustrate its meaning in terms of two aspects, one that is dark, and the other bright. The former can be understood as the negative aspect, and the latter, the positive aspect. He develops his arguments by analyzing the various novels, poems, and stories which reflect the Korean people's emotions. We can summarize his arguments as follows:[4]

Chun holds that the negative aspect of Hahn represents mainly these four meanings—*grudge*(怨), *chagrin* or *mortification*(寃), *lamentation*(嘆), and *sorrow*(悲哀). Regarding grudge, he argues that Hahn reflects the feeling of grudge, including curse, by introducing a Korean traditional proverb which says that "woman's Hahn forms hoarfrost even in summer."

He seeks the meaning of chagrin in the *Hanjungmanrok*(閑中漫錄), memoirs of Hyekyungkunghongsi(惠慶宮洪氏), who was the wife of Sado(思悼), a prince of the king Youngjo(英祖: 1694–1776) in the Chosun dynasty. As a prince, Sado had participated in the administration since he was 15 years old; however, his participation provoked serious conflict between king and prince.[5] Finally, the king ordered his people to put his son into a wooden rice-box. Sado dies in the box after one week. After his death, Sado's wife presents her feelings, in detail, through these memoirs. Chun summarizes the essence of her feelings as vexation.

Chun discerns the feeling of lamentation in some Korean traditional folk songs. One of the songs declares that the men who have a good destiny always enjoy their lives, while peasants have to work all day and night. This song reflects that it is meaningless, therefore, for the peasants to represent their Hahn. In this context, Chun argues that the feeling of lamentation is closely related to the concept of resignation or abandonment.

Finally, he explains the last negative aspect of Hahn as the feeling of sorrow, by analyzing the various Korean folk songs and poems. As an example, he introduces a poem, "A Lump of Sorrow" by Kim So-Wol(金素月: 1902–1934). According to a commentator of Korean literature, the sorrow explained in Kim's poem is the Korean people's typical emotion.[6]

The Korean people believe that this negative aspect of Hahn can cause a sickness called *Hwa-Byung*. *Hwa* means "fire," and *Byung* means "disease," in English. In his book, *Korean Values in the Age of Globalization*, Fred Alford considers Hwa-Byung a syndrome of anger and repression, introducing it as a special Korean syndrome in the DSM-IV.[7]

As the positive aspect of Hahn, Chun offers the feelings of "sentiment(情)" and "wish(願);" moreover, he emphasizes the characteristic of Hahn where affirmation and denial are mixed, as well as that of Hahn representing beauty. It is said that the Korean people are very sentimental. The famous Korean poet Cho Ji-Hoon(趙芝薫: 1920–1968) depicts the Korean people's lives as filled with many tears and regrets, in his poem "Wanhwasam(玩花衫)." In it, Cho explains the lots of love and Hahn as a special disease of the Korean people.[8] On the basis of this poem, Chun tries to explain the Hahn as something in the order of sentiment.

To better explain Chun's argument, we translate the concept of *Jeong*(情) as "sentiment." However, this concept, like Hahn, lacks an English equivalent. For example, a Korean-English dictionary defines Jeong with such words as "feeling," "sentiment," "emotion," and "warmhearted."[9] Therefore, this concept will be explained in more detail in the section discussing the "Emotional Dynamics of the Korean People."

Regarding Hahn as "wish," Chun says that it can also be a dream which is not realized. The situation in which our dream is not realized makes us unhappy. It may provoke some negative feelings such as grudge, chagrin, lamentation, and sorrow. However, we can also have another dream based on our ego ideal to solve our problem, as explained earlier. Because of this aspect, some people have tried to connect the meaning of Hahn to the feeling of wish. Thus, Chun says that "the meaning of Hahn is continually changed from the negative aspect into the positive aspect reflecting our wish."[10] In this context, Chun seeks to explain Hahn as a feeling where affirmation and denial are mixed. This implies that Hahn has not only the negative aspect but also the positive aspect.

In addition, Chun searches to find a beautiful element in the meaning of Hahn. In seeking this element, he analyzes the main characteristic of the voice in Korean traditional music, *Pansori*(판소리: a kind of opera). The voice of Pansori singers is very husky. It results from their efforts to *ferment* their feelings. The singers have to try to maintain the husky voice for a long time because this voice is suitable to represent the feeling of Hahn. Once their voices display a fermented quality, we say that they have achieved the sound which can move our emotions. Chun applies this effort to the understanding of Hahn. It reflects that the Korean people have tried to ferment their feelings such as grudge, chagrin, lamentation, and sorrow. And they wish to solve their problems by having another dream. This effort is enough to move our emotions; therefore, he argues that this effort can be regarded as a beautiful element of Hahn.

For understanding this beautiful element, we need additional explanations of the Korean Culture. There are so many fermented foods in Korea, especially in the southern area where the temperature is relatively higher than that of the northern area. The Korean people have developed lots of fermented foods for preventing spoiling. This is the scientific explanation. However, the Korean people also believe that poisonous substances in the food can be purified or neutralized by being fermented. This belief system is closely related to the Korean people's effort to ferment or purify their sorrow and grudge. Through this belief system, we can more clearly grasp the idea that the meaning of Hahn includes the wish to purify our problems. In this sense, an element of Hahn may be partly related to the concept of catharsis, which we have explained earlier.

To discover another beautiful element of Hahn, we need to consider it from a different aspect. This is the idea of waiting for something, or biding one's time. A Korean proverb observes that "time is a medicine to solve all our problems." This means that our problems may be forgotten with the passage of time. This view derives from the belief that there would be no problems if we forgot our sorrow. During the waiting, our problems may automatically disappear as time goes by. If not, we may find another dream by fermenting the problems. The concept of waiting is closely related to the wish as an element of Hahn. Thus, an element of Hahn is to endure through our problems by waiting for and wishing for a more desirable situation. Through endurance, our problems may be sublimated; therefore, Hahn can be also understood in terms of sublimation.

If we understand the meaning of Hahn as explained above, this concept is closely related to the concept of Sal. *Salpuri-Chum* is a compound word in which Chum is added to another compound word, Salpuri. *Chum* is a pure Korean word. It means "dance" in English.

Chum has its origins in the word *Chunam*(楸男).[11] *Chu* as a Chinese letter means a kind of walnut tree, and *Nam* means "man." However, the word meant "shaman" in the Korean kingdom of Koguryeo(高句麗: 37 BC–AD 668), although the reason that the Chinese letters were used for the word "shaman" is not clear. Chum is a noun, and its form of verb is Chuda. It has mainly two meanings; one is dance, and another, praise or applaud.[12] This implies that Chum is an activity to make people cheerful.

Thus, Salpuri-Chum means a dance for Puri Sal. The structure of Korean language is different from that of English. In this case, Sal is an object to Puri. And Puri as a gerund modifies the noun, Chum. In this sense, we can understand Salpuri-Chum as a dance for solving our Sal and Hahn. In other words, Salpuri-Chum is a dance which develops Salpuri to a form of art. Thus, we can say that Salpuri-Chum represents our desire and wish to solve our problems originating from our original limits for self-satisfaction and our discontents of civilization.

THEORY OF THE COLLECTIVE UNCONSCIOUS

In order to understand, in more detail, the meaning of Sal or Hahn, we need to examine some other things which we have not discussed yet. In doing so, the most important is to illustrate the essence of the collective unconscious of the Korean people, because this is the key to understanding the emotional dynamics of the Korean people. This key will provide us with many interesting ideas to interpret Salpuri-Chum in terms of psychoanalysis.

In considering the collective unconscious, we can begin with the theories set forth in Freud's *Group Psychology and the Analysis of the Ego*. In this work, he develops his theories by introducing the arguments of Gustave Le Bon (1841–1931), William McDougall (1871–1938), and Wilfred Trotter (1872–1939).

In *The Crowd: A Study of the Popular Mind*, Le Bon argues that an individual discards his own psychological impulses, and changes his attitude into the direction which his group requires.[13] In his book *The Group Mind*, McDougall points out that an individual may lose the function of his ego, which is the ability of emotional control.[14] Trotter's argument is stronger than those of Le Bon and McDougall. His book, *Instincts of the Herd in Peace and War*, emphasizes that an individual, as a herd animal, can expose his primitive instincts when he falls into a certain psychological condition of a crowd.[15]

By introducing these arguments, Freud supposes that an individual as a component of the group "has built up his ego ideal upon the most various models;" therefore "each individual…has a share in numerous group minds—those of his race, of his class, of his creed, of his nationality, etc."[16] The individual's share of the group mind can be understood in terms of the collective unconscious of the group members. Thus, this supposition can be very useful to understand the collective unconscious. However, in this study Freud focuses his attention only on the relations between the leader and the group members. He says that "the individual gives up his ego ideal and substitutes for it the group ideal as embodied in the leader."[17]

In this form, the Freudian theory of the collective unconscious could not be developed by his followers. Rather, it was studied by Carl Gustav Jung (1875–1961). Unlike Freud, he tries to find the essential elements of the collective unconscious in a certain trace originated from the ancestors, which he calls archetype.[18] However, Jung's theory of the collective unconscious was not accepted, particularly by Freudian psychoanalysts, because his concept of archetype was very ambiguous. But we can find some clues to understand the meaning of the collective unconscious in the object relation theory of psychoanalysis, which has been developed on the basis of Freud's theory.

As a physician, Freud first focused his attention on the instincts, because he believed that all human behaviors were basically motivated by the human being's animal nature. As a result, he asserted that there were two different instincts: one is an instinctual impulse to remove pain and to obtain pleasure, and the other, an aggressive impulse to inhibit pleasure-striving for the sake of self-preservation in reality.[19] The former is based on the pleasure principle, and the latter, on the reality principle. In this case, the aggressive impulse is understood as a response to the thwarting of pleasure seeking behavior. This explanation is reasonable; however, it does not provide us with clues to understand other phenomena such as "compulsive repetitions of unpleasant experiences, sadism, and especially self-destructive actions."[20]

Because of this problem, Freud tried to develop a new theory of human instinct. As a result, in his famous book, *Civilization and Its Discontents*, he argues that all human behavior is based on two main controversial instincts: Eros and Thanatos. The former can be understood as a love instinct to enhance and prolong life, and the latter, as a death or aggressive instinct to destroy life. Freud argues that "civilization is a process in the service of Eros, whose purpose is to combine single human individuals...into the unity of mankind," while "man's natural aggressive instinct, the hostility of each against all and of all against each, opposes this programme of civilization."[21] Here, the aggressive impulse is understood as an inborn drive, not a response to reality. If so, Freud's new theory of instinct allows us to understand sadism and self-destructive actions, which cannot be explained by the early theory of instinct.

Despite Freud's efforts to find the essential element motivating human behaviors, his instinct or drive theory was criticized by some psychoanalysts. This criticism was led by Harry Stack Sullivan (1892–1949). In his book *The Interpersonal Theory of Psychiatry*, Sullivan emphasized the cultural aspect of influence on personality, arguing that Freud focused only on the instinct without considering the influence of the outside world on the self.[22] This means that human behaviors are not motivated solely by the instincts, but they are also strongly influenced by environmental elements. We call this point of view *interpersonal psychoanalysis*. It had a great influence on American psychoanalysis, and contributed to the development of the "Neo-Freudian School," which emphasized cultural impact upon the formation of the unconscious.

We cannot disregard the environmental impact on human behavior; however, we also cannot deny the instinctual influences on our behavior. Consequently, interpersonal psychoanalysis began to be criticized by some psychoanalysts. For example, Harry Guntrip (1901–1975) argued that interpersonal psychoanalysis viewed "human nature as determined solely by culture pattern pressures," and that it "lost many of the fundamental discoveries made by Freud."[23] This view holds that our behaviors are influenced not only by the outside world but also by instincts.

Freud developed the concept of the unconscious, which had not been systematically discussed in the study of the human mind and behavior until his time. For him, the unconscious exists latently in our minds, and although we cannot lay hold of its existence, it absolutely controls our minds and behaviors. In other words, all our activities are motivated by the unconscious. This suggests that the purpose of psychoanalysis is to illuminate the unconscious. If so, then the most important task is to find the basic elements that influence the unconscious. As we discussed above, Freud first emphasized the instinctual elements, while Sullivan's interpersonal psychoanalysis began to emphasize the environmental elements. But many psychoanalysts came to recognize that we cannot fully understand the dynamics of the unconscious using only a single perspective.

In this context, a new theory began to be discussed. A leading psychoanalyst developing this new theory was Melanie Klein (1882–1960), in England. Unlike Freud and Sullivan, Klein did not separate instinct (or drive) from the object. In her article, "The Origins of Transference," she understands instinct as emotion directed toward others, in opposition to Freud's view that the body is the source of instinct.[24] For instance, the child begins to love the mother when she as the object is perceived as good; however, the child begins to hate her when she perceives the mother as bad.

This view sees love and hate as the basic (or master) passions formed in the object relations. Klein explains "all other passions, "such as envy, gratitude, guilt, grief, and mourning, as versions and combinations of the two master passions."[25] If so, we may say that the two instincts, love (Eros) and aggression (Thanatos), emphasized in Freud's drive theory cannot be understood as the fundamental elements controlling our emotions. Rather, Klein's concepts of love and hate are the paramount passions motivating our behaviors. In this respect we can say that Klein has changed the two Freudian concepts of instinct into the two fundamental passions formed in object relations. And this view paved a very useful way to construct object relation theory as the new stream of psychoanalysis.

According to object relation theory, the unconscious is formed and developed through the introjection and projection processes between the self and the object (or outside world). *Introjection* means the influence of the outside world on the self, whereas *projection* is the reflection of the self toward the object or outside world. Therefore, we act differently from each other according to the process of introjection and projection. However, if there are some common elements of the introjection and projection processes in the members of a group, we can find the collective unconscious of the group members. Furthermore, if we can illustrate the collective unconscious of the group members, we can understand the emotional dynamics which the group members manifest collectively. This is the basic assumption for studying the collective unconscious in terms of the object relation theory of psychoanalysis.

Chapter 2
EMOTIONAL DYNAMICS OF THE KOREAN PEOPLE

If we suppose that the Korean people have experienced some collective introjection and projection processes, the essential elements of the processes can be found in Korean history, philosophy, and culture. But before we consider such common introjection and projection processes of the Korean people, we should explain some peculiarities of their experiences. They have been strongly influenced by Confucianism and Buddhism. Also, they have suffered from many foreign invasions. Moreover, they could not avoid the legacy of an agrarian culture.

The nation of Korea has a very long history. Most Korean people believe that their country originated in the kingdom of Kochosun(古朝鮮), which was established in 2333 BC.[26] They are very proud of their history. In spite of this, historically their kingdoms were invaded many times by neighboring countries because their territory was very small, except for the kingdom of Koguryeo, which included the area of Manchuria beyond the Korean peninsula. To prevent invasions by the various foreign countries, they had to unite.

As you may know, Confucianism emphasizes human relationships. In Confucianism, the final judgment for discerning between good and bad is based on the relations between king and subject, parents and son or daughter, husband and wife, adults and children, and between friends. We call these relations *Samgang*(三綱: the Three Bonds in human relations) and *Oryun*(五倫: the Five Moral Rules in human relations).[27] These moral rules are very hierarchical in the social order.

Buddhism also had a strong influence on the Korean people's belief system. According to Buddhism, every existent is closely related to every other existent. We call this "the theory of interdependent arising." This theory proposes that "if there is this, there is that, and if there is not this, there is not that."[28] According to this theory, things are not completely separate from each other, but are interconnected. Thus, this theory can be partly related to monism in western philosophy.

It is said that the ultimate question of western philosophy is "who I am." This can be regarded as one of main reasons why individualism developed in western societies. But the ultimate question of Asian philosophy, rooted in Confucianism and Buddhism, is "who we are." Thus, collectivism (or groupism) developed in Asian societies, where the ruling ideology is based on Confucianism and Buddhism. Consider that the communist revolution first occurred in Russia, and expanded to Asian societies. Why did the revolution occur in the non-western societies, contrary to Marx's expectation? This answer may lie in the collectivism of Asian peoples. In fact, Marx was the first western philosopher who reshaped the ultimate question of western philosophy into that of Asian philosophy.[29]

Korea is a typical agrarian nation, although it is very mountainous. Farming requires all family members and village people to work together. This also is one of main reasons that collectivism developed in Korean society. Moreover, the agrarian culture likely promotes purpose-oriented behavior, because the people focus their attention on the harvest resulting from their efforts. Thus, the object is emphasized in languages influenced by agrarian cultures.

For example, the structure of the Korean languages based on the agrarian culture first requires an object, not a subject. This structure is absolutely different from that of a language which first requires a subject. In general, the subject is most important in a nomadic society, because each person has to keep his own animals, and move them around the wide grassy areas where they graze. This may be also one of reasons why individualism has developed in western societies based on the nomadic culture.

We can discuss the peculiarities of Korean history, philosophy, and culture, from various points of view. However, insofar as we focus on the collective unconscious of the Korean people, we can point out the several common characteristics reflecting their emotional dynamics. These will provide us with some useful clues to more deeply understand Salpuri-Chum. In this context, we can summarize the essential elements of the emotional characteristics existing in the Korean people's collective unconscious as follows:

First, most Korean people have Hahn, explained in the beginning of this chapter. Women's Hahn especially was more serious than men's in the traditional Korean society which allowed the rise of the supremacy of men. This Hahn originated from their history and philosophy. Throughout the numerous foreign invasions and civil wars, many people died. The lower class people were oppressed by the higher class people because Confucianism as a ruling ideology for a long time emphasized the hierarchical order of human relationships, the relations between supremacy and submission. In addition, most people suffered from poverty. These circumstances were enough to provoke Hahn in the Korean people.

Second, most Korean people are very emotional. Therefore, they often cry or are angry; but they also frequently laugh. This is the reason why there are two contradictory aspects (negative and positive) of Hahn, as explained earlier. Dream or wish as the positive aspect of Hahn is derived from the Korean people's *Heung* (merriment), which habituates them to easy laughter.

As you may know, most Korean people are very merry. They enjoy singing. There are many amateur singing contests, as well as the karaoke stores (Noraebang: 노래방 in Korean), where people can sing the songs they want even today. They like to pacify their stresses by singing various songs. They recharge their energy through the so-called Heung; and further, they want to transform their anger into Heung. Through Heung, they pacify their sorrow and anger, and try to overcome those negative feelings. They continually try to solve their problems and create their new destinies, yet they express the feeling of sorrow derived from their unhappiness. This reflects the two faces of their emotional dynamics.

We also need to explain the role of anger. If we are angry about a certain situation, the anger may have two functions. One is to nullify our sorrow through the catharsis, because the anger also may be a way for catharsis. Another function is to move us to find a solution to the problem. If there is no stress, we have no need for anger. Of course, a situation having no stress at all is that of death. Anger, therefore, can be connected to an effort to change the situation. We cannot be moved to change our situation if we do not feel anger. Thus, anger sometimes functions positively. For instance, we may say that the rapid economic development of Korean society derived from the Korean people's anger toward their poverty.

Third, most Korean people have a quick perception of other people and their situations. This, of course, is derived from the fact that they are very sensitive or emotional. However, this was also derived from their history, which was marked by many wars. Survival in dangerous situations requires quick decisions. Therefore, their emotional representation is improvisatorial. This reflects that the most Korean people are not logical; rather, their behavior is based on the improvisatorial emotion.

Fourth, most Korean people are very cohesive. This results from the philosophy and culture which has greatly influenced their behaviors. In this coherence, there is no strict boundary between the self and others. Therefore, they always emphasize the concept of "we." This trend is manifested even in some artistic performances. For example, the audiences and the performers are not separated from each other, especially in most of the traditional plays and art performances. Of course, we can say that this is also derived from their sensibility.

Through these characteristics, we can understand, in more detail, the essential elements of the Korean people's collective unconscious. However, we have to discuss one more concept of the feeling or passion in order to understand more fully their emotional dynamics. This is the concept of *Jeong*. Korean people say that they have a lot of Jeong. When we discussed the concept of Hahn, we interpreted Jeong as "feeling" or "sentiment." However, strictly speaking, the word, Jeong, like Hahn, also lacks a direct English equivalent. In Jeong are the two controversial concepts, love and hate. In the western psychoanalytic tradition, especially in the object relation theory, love and hate—as the paramount passions— are understood separately from each other. But in the Korean tradition, love and hate are understood in a mixed form.

For the Korean people, the feeling of hate cannot exist alone. It may be understood as a reactionary feeling against the feeling of love. When our love is rejected by its object, we begin to hate the object as a reaction. Therefore, the feelings of love and hate are two sides of the same coin. This means that there is no feeling of hate if there is no feeling of love. If so, the feeling of hate also includes that of love. In other words, hate can be understood as another aspect of love.

In this context, the Korean concept of Jeong can be understood as a mixed feeling. For example, a Korean proverb says: "We laugh because of Jeong, and we cry because of Jeong." Many Korean people hesitate to leave their love object even if their love object rejects their love. In other words, they do not leave their love object even though they hate their love object. This is very paradoxical.

Lee Jo-Nyun(李兆年: 1269–1343), a Korean poet in the kingdom of Koryeo(高麗: 918–1392) laments in his poem, "Dajeongga(多情歌: Song of the Much Jeong)" as follows: "In a deep night where the flowers of a pear tree reflect the light of moon and where the milky way runs, a cuckoo may not know the mind of spring sinking into a branch of the tree; however, I cannot sleep because of too much Jeong becoming a disease."[30]

After reading this poem, we may simply understand the Jeong as something sentimental. In this sense, we can interpret the last sentence as follows; "I get a disease because I am so sentimental or emotional; thus, I cannot sleep." However, if we consider the situation which he explains, we can interpret it more clearly. The scenery which he explains is very beautiful; therefore, he loves the scenery. Despite this, he simultaneously feels sorrow because he loves it too much. He describes this kind of feeling as a disease, causing his inability to sleep. If so, we can understand the situation in which too much love may provoke sorrow.

Kim Yong-Shin in his book, *The Ego Ideal, Ideology and Hallucination*, also explains that too much love between mother and son is likely to be connected to a regressive attachment.[31] In this case, the regressive attachment can be related to the disease mentioned in the above poem. This connection, then, can be seen as a negative reflection on too much love. In this way, we see that we can hate an object because we love it too much. This implies that love and hate can coexist in our minds for the same object.

As mentioned earlier, Klein points out that there can be various passions which are combinations of love and hate. Despite this view, she does not fully explain some special patterns in which the two master passions, love and hate, coexist. Her explanation focuses only on the fact that all other passions originate from the two paramount passions. However, when we consider the concept of Jeong, we can find one very interesting fact—namely, that most Korean people do not understand Joung as a sub-passion of love and hate. Rather, they think that love and hate cannot be separated from each other; therefore they believe that Jeong is the Korean people's main or paramount passion, which includes simultaneously love and hate.

In fact, it is very difficult to illustrate systematically the meaning of Jeong in terms of the object relation theory, because western psychoanalysis does not identify a particular passion which corresponds to Jeong. However, insofar as we focus our attention on the understanding of the Korean people's unconscious, the theoretical debate to define the meaning of Jeong may not be a matter of serious concern. The more important thing is to understand that the Korean people's emotional dynamics are based on the Jeong where love and hate coexist without being separated from each other.

The Korean people's recognition of this kind of mixed feeling may have contributed to the development of monism. Conversely, this recognition might be derived from the Asian tradition influenced by monism, or the theory of interdependent arising in Buddhism. In any case, most Korean people generally hesitate to discern clearly the different elements in a phenomenon because they feel that all the elements are closely related to each other. If we understand this kind of attitude, we can more easily understand the Korean people's emotional dynamics. And if we understand the essence of their emotional dynamics, we can more deeply understand their activities reflecting their unconscious.

NOTES

1. *Chinese Dictionary (네이버 한자사전)*, s.v. "煞," accessed October 19, 2016, http://hanja.naver.com/hanja?q=%E7%85%9E.
2. *The Great Korean Dictionary*(큰사전), comp. Association for Studying the Hangul (Seoul: Eulyumunhwasa(을유문화사), 1957), s.v. "살" (Sal).
3. Ibid., s.v. "한" (Hahn).
4. Yi-Du Chun, *A Study on the Structure of Hahn* (Seoul: Munhak & Jisung, 1993), 20–52.
5. Yong-Shin Kim, *EIIH*, 87.
6. Yi-Du Chun, *Structure of Hahn*, 29.
7. Fred Alford, Korean Values in the Age of Globalization, trans. Kyung-Tae Nam (Seoul: Greenbee, 2000), 130–31. DSM-IV refers to the Diagnostic and Statistical Manual of Mental Disorders, 4th ed., published by the American Psychiatric Association; also known as DSM-IV-TR.
8. Yi-Du Chun, *Structure of Hahn*, 35.
9. *Si-Sa Elite Concise Korean-English Dictionary*, 2nd ed. (Seoul: Si-sa-yong-o-sa, 1992), s.v. "情" (Jeong).
10. Yi-Du Chun, *Structure of Hahn*, 41.
11. Byung-Ok Lee, *History of the Korean Dance* (Seoul: Minsokwon, 2013), 23.
12. *Great Korean Dictionary*, s.v. "추다" (Chuda).
13. Gustave Le Bon, *The Crowd: A Study of the Popular Mind* (United States: Digireads.Com, 2008), quoted in Sigmund Freud, *Group Psychology and the Analysis of the Ego*, trans. and ed. James Strachey (New York: W.W. Norton, 1959), 4–13. Also see Yong-Shin Kim, *False Image of Leadership* (Seoul: Acaone, 2016), 107.
14. William McDougall, *The Group Mind: a sketch of the principles of colletive* [sic] *psychology, with some attempt to apply them to the interpretation of national life and character.* (Cambridge: University Press / Ann Arbor, MI: University of Michigan Library, 1920) [reprint], quoted in Freud, *Group Psychology*, 15–18. Also see Yong-Shin Kim, *False Image of Leadership*, 108.

15. Wilfred Trotter, *Instincts of the Herd in Peace and War*, quoted in Freud, *Group Psychology*, 19. Also see Yong-Shin Kim, *False Image of Leadership*, 108.
16. Freud, *Group Psychology*, 61.
17. Ibid.
18. Anthony Storr, *Jung* (London: Fontana Press, 1973), 39–61.
19. Sigmund Freud, "Beyond the Pleasure Principle," *S.E.*, vol.18, *1920–1922, Beyond the Pleasure Principle, Group psychology, and other works* (1955), 1–64.
20. Albert Bandura, *Aggression: Social Learning Analysis* (Englewood Cliffs, NJ: Prentice Hall, 1973), 12.
21. Sigmund Freud, *Civilization and Its Discontents*, trans. and ed., James Strachey (New York: W.W. Norton, 1961), 69.
22. Harry S. Sullivan, *The Interpersonal Theory of Psychiatry* (New York: Norton, 1953), quoted in Greenberg and Mitchell, *Object Relations*, 79–115.
23. Harry Guntrip, *Personality Structure and Human Interaction: the Developing Synthesis of Psychoanalysis* (New York: International Universities Press, 1961), 354.
24. Melanie Klein, "The Origin of Transference," in *The Writings of Melanie Klein*, (London: Hogarth Press, 1975), 3:51.
25. Alford, *Melanie Klein*, 8.
26. *Doopedia, s.v.* "고조선" (Kochosun), accessed November 10, 2016, http://terms.naver.com/entry.nhn?docId=1062323&cid=40942&categoryId=33374.
27. The three bonds of *Samgang* are: 1) *Goonwisingang*(君爲臣綱), the bond between the king and the subject; 2) *Boowijagang*(父爲子綱), the bond between parents and children; and 3) *Boowiboogang*(夫爲婦綱), the bond between husband and wife. The five moral rules of *Oryun* are: 1) *Boojayoochin*(父子有親), the moral rule for affection between father and son; 2) *Goonsinyooi*(君臣有義), the moral rule for loyalty between king and subject; 3) *Boobooyoobyeol*(夫婦有別), the moral rule for distinction between husband and wife; 4) *Jangyooyooseo*(長幼有序), the moral rule for order between adults and children; and 5) *Boongwooyoosin*(朋友有信), the moral rule for trust between friends.
28. *Great Dictionary of Wonbulgyo*(원불교대사전), s.v. "연기론," accessed November 10, 2016, http://terms.naver.com/entry.nhn?docId=2112867&cid=50765&categoryId=50778.
29. Yong-Shin Kim, *Psychology Meets the Korean People* (Seoul: Sidam, 2010), 89.
30. *Doopedia*, s.vv. "다정기" (Dajeongga), "이조년" (Lee Jo-Nyun), accessed October 19, 2016, http://terms.naver.com/entry.nhn?docId=1135444&cid=40942&categoryId=33382.
31. Yong-Shin Kim, *EIIH*, 90–98.

Chapter Three

Shamanic Ritual as a Way to Expel Evil Spirits

THE KOREAN PEOPLE'S TRADITIONAL PERCEPTION
OF DEATH

In his book *Primitive Culture*, Edward B. Tyler notes that ancient peoples thought that the soul of a dead person had some influences on the living person's life.[1] This idea also prevailed in traditional Korean society. As mentioned earlier, the Korean people's belief system was strongly influenced by Confucianism and Buddhism. It can be understood as the *introjection* process. Or conversely, their reactions to circumstances may have contributed to the development of Confucianism and Buddhism. This can be understood as the *projection* process. In any case, the people's thinking about the relations between the dead person and the living person was more closely related to Confucianism than Buddhism, because Confucianism more strongly emphasized ancestor worship than did Buddhism.

In fact, the ancestor worship emphasized in Confucianism originated from the ancient people's perception of death in Asian society. For them, the human being has three basic elements: *Hon*(魂), *Baek*(魄), and *Yookche*(肉體). Hon means "spirit," while Baek means "energy for the movement of the body." And Yookche means "body."[2] In this case, death means that Hon and Baek leave the body. The Emperor *Youngrakje*(永樂帝: 1402–1424) of the Myung(明) dynasty in China ordered forty-two scholars to edit the famous Chinese book about human nature, *Sunglidaejeon*(性理大全: Xingli daquan), which maintains that Hon and Baek leave the body after death.[3]

In this belief, Hon and Baek function for a long time after death although the body easily disappears. This suggests that life continues although the body disappears. This may derive from the people's wish to live forever. However, this also supports a belief that the Hon and Baek of the dead person may have an influence on the living person. This belief promoted the veneration of ancestors, and developed the memorial ceremonies for the dead.

Of course, Hon and Baek do not exist forever. They also disappear after some period of time. According to Confucianism, they disappear about after four generations (about 100 to 120 years). Thus, people want to perform the memorial ceremony every year only for their ancestors as far back as their great-grandparents (the parents of their grandparents).

In the Chinese tradition, the Hon and Baek of the dead person are expressed as *Gwisin*(鬼神: "ghost"). However, the Chinese people classified Gwisin into the three types: *Sinlyung*(神靈: a god or a kind of divine being), *Chosangsin*(祖上神: god of ancestor), and Gwisin, a sorrowful ghost.[4] Sinlyung, as the highest class, controls a certain area such as a mountain and a river. In this case, it is not called a ghost, but it becomes an object respected by all the people. The god of ancestor is the next class. It is an object respected only by its descendants as a transcendental being. And Gwisin of the third class is a sorrowful soul. This ghost has some regrettable problems or repressed desires which were not solved in this world. It can be understood as an evil spirit in the western tradition.

In Freudian psychoanalysis, evil spirits or demons are derived from guilt. The primal father dominated all women in his primitive group; however, "One day the brothers who had been driven out came together, killed and devoured their father and so made an end of the patriarchal horde."[5] After killing their father, they could gain satisfaction, yet they suffered remorse for their crime; thus originated guilt.

Patrick McNamara says, "At the level of the individual psyche, Freud would argue, guilt arises in the desire to kill the father so as to have exclusive access to the mother, that is, the Oedipal complex."[6] The guilt feeling provokes fear of the soul of the primal father. Indeed, to the aforementioned brothers, the soul of the father can cause harm by becoming an evil spirit. Therefore, desiring to be free of such evil spirits, ancient people created shamanic rituals and religions to exorcise evil spirits, and they wanted to expiate their guilt in the process.

The above understanding based on guilt cannot be directly applied to the traditional Korean society without cultural adaptation. The Korean people, like the Chinese people, believed that the soul of the dead person continued to exist in the sky—even as his body lay buried in the earth—permitting the soul of the dead to influence the destiny of the living. Nobody wants to die; thus, death may provoke regrets. Of course, the soul (Hon and Baek) which becomes Sinlyung and Chosangsin is not regretful. But the soul which becomes Gwisin with regrets can come to hate and hurt the living, while wandering in the middle of the sky. This is the evil spirit, a dead person's soul causing harm to a living person.

This understanding is closely related to Westermarck's opinion introduced in Freud's *Totem and Taboo*. He says, as follows:

> Death is commonly regarded as the gravest of all misfortunes; hence the dead are believed to be exceedingly dissatisfied with their fate. According to primitive ideas, a person only dies if he is killed—by magic if not by force—and such a death naturally tends to make the soul revengeful and ill-tempered. It is envious of the living and is longing for the company of its old friends; no wonder, then, that it sends them diseases to cause their death...But the notion that the disembodied soul is on the whole a malicious being...is also, no doubt, intimately connected with the instinctive fear of the dead, which is in its turn the outcome of the fear of death.[7]

In the Korean tradition, the soul of the dead person is likely to influence those who are closely related to them. The ghosts who have grudges or regrets, in particular, are likely to cause harm to their living relatives. Therefore, in the Korean tradition, as in the Chinese tradition, the fear of the souls of the dead who have regrets or grudges also gave rise to the veneration of ancestors or dead persons, as well as the fear of demons and ghosts.

This also relates to the Freudian psychoanalytic viewpoint in *Totem and Taboo*.[8] With such fears, the ancient Korean people desired a way to escape from them; that is, they sought a means to prevent the dead from influencing the living. This desire to be free of fear drove the creation of shamanic rituals in traditional Korean society.

As mentioned earlier, not all souls of the dead become evil spirits. In the Korean belief system, some souls can ascend to the highest position in the sky, comparable to the heaven of Judeo-Christian tradition. The souls of these dead do not hurt the living; rather, they solve the problems of the living. They also can fulfill wishes.

Not surprisingly, the Korean people want the ascension of their ancestors' souls because these souls may aid rather than harm the living. Seeking means by which people could aid their ancestors' souls in their ascension led to geomantic studies, theories of divination based on topography. The Korean people call this theory *Poong-Soo*(風水). Poong as a Chinese letter means "wind," and Soo means "water." Wind and water have a strong influence on the places where we live. Thus, Poong-Soo has been used to find good places even for burying the dead, namely, places that would help the souls of the dead ascend to the highest position in the sky. This type of good place is called *Myungdang*(明堂).[9] Myung as a Chinese letter means "light," and Dang, "house" or "place."

In the Korean tradition, death means "return," unlike in the western tradition where death is conceived of as "passing away." For the ancient Korean people, the souls of the dead return to their original home, the highest place in the sky, because the souls of the living originate there. The original home can be compared with the concept of primary narcissistic perfection (mother's womb) in Freudian psychoanalysis. However, souls with Hahn do not return to their original home until the Hahn is resolved. In this case, the soul of the dead person wanders in the middle of the sky, causing harm to the living related to him in this world. This harm is seen as a sign to the living for help in solving the dead person's Hahn.

The blurring of the realms of the living and dead is reflected in the Korean people's unconscious to solve the Hahn of the dead. In civilization, most people are unable to realize complete satisfaction; therefore most people may possess Hahn. For the Korean people, Hahn is derived from poverty, oppression, ignorance, and the like.[10] In particular, women in the Korean traditional society were oppressed in the name of Confucian values, which focused on the life of men. Thus, we may conclude that Korean women are more likely to have Hahn than men.

A famous Korean poet, Ko Un(高銀: 1933–) says, "Korean people are born from the womb of Hahn, grow by eating the mother's milk of Hahn, living by enduring Hahn, and die by leaving Hahn."[11] Despite this situation, most of Korean people have a strong desire to resolve their Hahn. If they do not do so in this world, they will want to resolve their Hahn after death. In this sense, we may add one more sentence to Ko's poem as follows; "Therefore, the Korean people's Hahn and its resolution continues even after death." This reflects the unconscious desire of the Korean people to change their destiny.

Most Korean people believed that misfortunes such as disease and suffering were likely caused by an evil spirit. And such an evil spirit was believed to be the soul of a dead person who has Hahn in this world. Therefore, to rid an individual of the misfortune he suffers, the evil spirit's Hahn must be resolved. This is done through various Guts, expelling the evil spirit.

GUT AS SHAMANIC RITUAL FOR SALPURI

In the traditional Korean society, the people's wish to solve their Sal or Hahn was represented in a shamanic ritual. When we cannot solve our problems in reality, we may try to solve them even in our hallucinations, as psychoanalytic theory explains. Also, we may pray to some transcendental power for solving these problems. Praying to a god may derive from the belief that our destinies depend upon a god's will. In this context, a Korean psychiatrist argues as follows:

> Fundamental nature of shamanism in Korea likewise in the other cultures is so called "projective cultural system." All of the human problems such as life and

death, fortune and misfortune, psychological and physical distresses are so intimately attributed to the supernatural causes that inner problems of an individual are projected unto the will of supernatural beings. Hence, they relieve their anxieties rather by treating the supernatural beings, than by confronting with the problems as their own ones and trying to gain insight to the inner causes and coping with their problems.[12]

If we suppose that the projective activity based on shamanism is also understood as a human effort to solve our problems, this cannot be seen simply as regressive behavior. This activity is, in fact, based on our wish not only to overcome our original limits, but also to pacify our sorrow derived from civilization. Therefore, the Korean shamanic ritual as a way to solve the Sal or Hahn of the Korean people will provide us with useful ideas to characterize Salpuri-Chum originated from the ritual.

In Korean shamanism, we hold the shamanic ritual to solve Sal or Hahn. *Gut* is a pure Korean word. Most Korean scholars argue that Gut means Puri. For example, Lee Neung-Hwa interprets Gut as a ritual to solve Sal or Hahn, and to pray for happiness and fortune.[13] Yoo Dong-Sik, following G. J. Ramstedt's argument, tries to find the origin of the word Gut from the words meaning "happiness" or "fortune" in Altaic languages, such as *Kutu* in Tungusic, *Qutug* in Manchurian, and *Qut* in Turkish. Therefore, he interprets the meaning of Gut as a shamanic ritual for happiness or fortune.[14]

In addition to the above meanings, Gut has another meaning. This meaning refers to an "interesting and loud performance or play."[15] In traditional society, Gut was a very important and interesting ritual; thus, many people wanted to watch the process of Gut. The shaman conducting Gut narrated or incanted very loudly. Therefore, Gut has also come to mean the performance or the play.

There have been many gods who control their own territories in Korean tradition. For example, the ancient Korean people asked the god of the sea to solve problems pertaining to the sea, and the god of the mountain to solve problems related to the mountain. Famous historical persons are also respected as gods after their deaths, and people pray to these famous souls for help in solving their present problems.[16] Moreover, the soul of an ancestor who returned to the highest place in the sky also can be a god who can solve the problems of his descendants.

A shaman is a person who can communicate with the gods. He or she conveys the messages of gods to the people, and the wishes of the people to the gods. For fulfilling these tasks, the Korean shaman believed that he first of all had to have an ability to communicate with gods. However, this ability cannot be obtained by the human will. Only gods can give the ability to a special person.

Therefore, a person who is to be a shaman first gets a disease. This disease is hardly remedied by the medical treatment developed by human beings. In this case, many people began to believe that this disease may be *Sin-Byung*(神病), a disease originating from a god. If so, it is remedied only after the sick person has performed a Gut to accept the spirit of the god. This is called *Jupsin*(接神)-*Gut*. If the person has successfully completed the Jupsin-Gut, he or she can finally become a shaman who can communicate with gods.

In general, most Korean shamans can communicate with various gods. However, the shaman can communicate more easily with the god who gave him the disease than with other gods. Therefore, each shaman can get a special ability in keeping with the god whom he accepted. For example, the shaman who accepts a death ancestor as a god can more easily convey the family wishes to the god. And if the shaman accepted a god of the sea, the shaman, through a Gut, more easily solve problems related to the sea.

Once a person accepts a god, he or she has to make a *Sindang*(神堂), a room or small house where the god comes down, and pray to the god every day. Under this condition, the shaman has to learn the incantation, music, and dance for conducting Gut related to his or her special ability, from the shaman who has already finished Jupsin-Gut. The shaman's customs are quite varied, according to the god whom he or she accepted, as well as according to regions.

In Korean society, most shamans are female. They are called *Mudang*(巫堂). The numbers of male shamans are relatively small. They are called *Barksoo*. "巫" as a Chinese letter means shamanism. Its Korean pronunciation is "Mu." The pronunciation of this letter is same as that of the letter "舞," meaning dance. According to one study, "舞" is a hieroglyph describing the situation in which a shaman dances. And "巫" is a hieroglyph describing the situation in which a shaman dances in a shrine.[17] This means that shaman and dance are closely related to each other in the ancient Asian society. Moreover, the pronunciation of both words is same in Korean.

Dang as a Chinese letter means house, as mentioned earlier. Thus, Mudang literally means a person in shamanic house, while the word Barksoo has no equivalent Chinese word. Hence, it is said that the word may be derived from some other Chinese words whose pronunciations are similar to Barksoo, such as *Barksoo*(拍手: handclap), *Barksa*(博士: person who has lots of knowledge), and *Jumsa*(占士: fortune-teller).[18]

Mudang and Barksoo have their own language which the ordinary people cannot understand. But their language is not impromptu. It is another expression of the existing words. Thus, it can be understood as a kind of jargon. This may result from their belief that they have to have their own language in order to communicate with the gods.[19]

There is also another type of shaman in Korean society called *Dangol*(당골 or 단골). Choi Nam-Sun(崔南善: 1890–1957), a noted writer and historian, suggests that Dangol originated from the word *Tengri* in the Altai language, which means the god in heaven.[20] Although Dangols are understood as a kind of shaman, they have not experienced the so-called Jupsin and do not need to have a Sindang. They do direct the various shamanic rituals; however, they act only as helpers or assistants of the shaman in the Gut. Their social status is relatively low and is transmitted from generation to generation. In this sense, Dangol can be understood as a priest, as explained by Max Weber in his book, *On Charisma and Institution Building*.[21]

There are various types of Guts according to the purpose and special culture of the region; thus, it is very complicated to explain all the kinds of Gut in Korea. However, these can be broadly classified into two basic types. In the first type, the Korean people pray for dead persons. Through this Gut, it is hoped that the dead person can get to the highest part of the sky, so they can solve or pacify their grudges remaining from this world. In the second type of Gut, the people pray for the fortune of living persons. Through this Gut, they pray not only for fortune, wealth, and health, of the individual person, but also for fortune or prosperity for the village and country.[22]

The various Guts can be also classified in two other ways. One aims at praying to the good gods for happiness or fortune, while the other focuses on the prevention of the influences of evil spirits. In the former case, the shaman simply prays that the good gods give us what we want. In the latter case, however, the shaman concentrates on expelling the evil spirits which may harm living persons, by solacing their grudges or Hahn in this world. We generally call this type *Salpuri-Gut*.

Yet such classifications may be rather meaningless, because the main purpose of Gut in praying to a god is focused on the happiness or fortune of the living person. Because Gut is used to expel an evil spirit, this is at the same time a way to find happiness for living persons. Accordingly, we can understand all types of Gut as shamanic rituals for the happiness of living persons. However, if we emphasize the meaning of Salpuri in Gut, its main task may be to expel evil spirits. In particular, if we want to analyze Gut to find the original meaning of Salpuri-Chum, it is very helpful to understand the structure or form of the so-called Salpuri-Gut. To this end, we will discuss mainly Salpuri-Gut in this section.

The structure of gut is very complicated; however, it can be divided into three processes.[23] The shaman begins with a process to call forth the god or evil spirit. Next, the shaman amuses the god and asks him to solve the various problems. In the case of an evil spirit, the shaman conducts a procedure to solace the evil spirit by promising to solve his grudge or Hahn left in the world. Finally, the shaman performs a rite of farewell to send the god back to the place from which it came. In the case of an evil spirit, the final process is to send it to a higher part of the sky by solving its Hahn or grudge. If the evil spirit's grudge or Hahn is fully resolved through Gut, its soul goes to the highest place in the sky. For the Korean people, the evil spirit can no longer hurt the living once its Hahn is resolved through the Gut.

In the typical Salpuri-Gut, the shaman generally dances with a piece of fabric. This piece of fabric, especially white fabric, represents the soul.[24] The use of the fabric varied across different regions. For example, the shaman knots and unknots the fabric in a certain regions (see Photo 1). We call it *Gopuri*(고푸리).[25] *Go* is a pure Korean word and means "knot," while Puri means "solve" or "unknot," as explained earlier. The knot symbolizes the Hahn of the dead person. Accordingly, the performance to unknot the knots in the fabric symbolizes the process whereby the Hahn is resolved.

In another Gut, the shaman splits the fabric into two pieces (see Photo 2). In this Gut two different colored fabrics, yellow linen and white silk, are generally used. The linen represents the way the living person will meet his fortune. The white fabric represents the way the dead may enter the highest place in the sky. The fabrics thus symbolize this world, and the world of the dead. The shaman splits the fabric to open the way through which the soul of the living or the dead can obtain happiness.[26] We call this *Gilgareum*(길가름), which is a pure Korean word. *Gil* means "way" or "road," and *Gareum*(가름) means "split."[27] The fabric colors can vary by region and shaman.

Shamans may also use coin-shaped papers, called *Jijeon*(紙錢), connected together. *Ji* means "paper," and *Jeon*, "coin." The shaman ties the pieces of paper on two bamboo swords, and dances, shaking the swords with both hands.[28] The paper represents money, and the fluttering pieces of coin-shaped paper is meant to soothe the soul of the dead person, making it happy.

The fabric is a primitive banner representing our desires, expectations, and dreams. Thus it can symbolize the ego ideal. It is also a banner representing our sorrowful minds suffering from reality. We can find this understanding in a poem titled "Flag," by Yoo Chi-Hwan (柳致環: 1908–1967), a famous Korean poet. He writes:

> It is a shout without sound
> And an eternal handkerchief of nostalgia
> Waving toward the end of blue sea
> A pure heart, like a wave, flutters
> And an indefinable sadness, like a white heron, spreads its wings
> At the top of the pure and straight ideology
> Ah!
> Who is the person
> Knowing first the way to hang
> Such a sorrowful mind in the air?"[29]

Lee Eun-Joo offers another interpretation of the fabric. The fabric is seen as a necessary primitive invention for human life, from birth to death. Fabric is a diaper and a baby carrier. Fabric is used as a banner (*Manjang*: 만장in Korean), where the living may write their wishes for the dead. Fabric protects our body; it can provide us with the space upon which we may represent our wishes. Lee points out that the pieces of fabric used in Guts are symbols of our lives.[30] In this light, the pieces of fabric represent our souls because the souls symbolize our lives.

The interplay of destiny and creativity had defined the variety of Guts in the Korean shamanic tradition. For the Korean people, human beings are in part fated beings because their destiny is strongly influenced by the dead, e.g., Hahn, and the environment, e.g., Myungdang. But the Korean people also believe that humanity is creative, because they try to change destiny through the use of shamanic rituals. This interplay between destiny and creativity exemplifies that lack of distinction between the living and the dead in the Korean traditions.

SINAWI RHYTHM AS THE MUSICAL ACCOMPANIMENT OF GUT

All types of Gut have been performed or conducted with Sinawi rhythm. Therefore, it is very important to understand the rhythm in illustrating that the main characteristic of Salpuri-Chum originated from Salpuri-Gut. In doing so, we need first understand the peculiarities of the Korean traditional music. As far as we focus on the musical accompaniment of Salpuri-Chum, these peculiarities can be summarized as follows:

First, Korean traditional music has only five musical scales, unlike western music, which has seven scales. This is derived from the theory of *Yin-Yang*(陰陽) and *Ohaeng*(五行) in Asian philosophy. It is very difficult to understand the concept of Yin and Yang; however, it can be simply explained as minus and plus energy in terms of western scientific point of view. The concept of Ohaeng refers to the movements of five fundamental elements in the universe. According to the theory of Yin-Yang and Ohaeng, all beings are made by the five fundamental elements: *Hwa*(火: fire), *Soo*(水: water), *Mok*(목: wood), *Geum*(金: steel), and *To*(土: earth). And all creations or changes depend upon the movement of Yin and Yang energy. This is the main reason why the Korean music has the five musical scales.

Second, the tempo of Korean traditional music is relatively slow. For example, the tempo is three or four times slower than that of the metronomic-based so-called moderato in western music. Han Myung-Hee, a theorist of Korean traditional music, says that the speed of the Western metronome is based on the pulse, while the speed of Korean traditional music is based on respiration.[31] It is a very interesting explanation. The Korean word *Han-soom*(한숨) is composed of *Han*, meaning "one," and *Soom*, meaning "breath." This word has two meanings: One is just "a breath," and the other "a deep breath" or "sigh." The latter is closely related to the meaning of Hahn, because people who have some sorrows often sigh over some regrettable situation, or over their fates in general. In fact, the pronunciation of Han is same as that of Hahn. In this light, the breath is seen as closely related to the Korean people's feelings. If so, the above interpretation of musical tempos may be more understandable.

Third, despite this slow tempo, the speed gradually increases and becomes very fast in the final part, although the final part is relatively short. This may derive from the Korean people's merriment, explained earlier. Most Korean people like to enjoy the climax of music in the last part. They want to pacify their Hahn and feel a catharsis through the fastest speed.

Fourth, Korean traditional music lacks a specific harmonic system. In western music, the harmony among the various musical tones is very important. However, this kind of harmony is not important in Korean music. According to Han, this results from the difference between the ways in which western people and Korean people understand the world. For instance, western people like to see a thing analytically by separating the various elements in it from each other, while the Korean people prefer to see it in its totality, without separating the elements from each other.[32] This may be the result of the Asian monism explained earlier.

Fifth, Korean traditional music likes to use the three-beat system. As you may know, the traditional music in China and Japan like to use the two-beat system. Han tries to explain this difference in the Korean People's outlook on the universe, seeing it in terms of the three elements—sky, earth and human being.[33] Apart from this interpretation, most Korean people, in fact, like the number three.

In addition to these five characteristics, we may point out a number of other elements of Korean music. However, these five main characteristics are enough to provide us with very useful ideas to understand the essence of Sinawi rhythm. This is because these five elements are more emphasized in Sinawi rhythm.

All shamanic rituals contain song and dance because these are techniques to invoke the gods. Music, song, and dance, then, are necessary elements of shamanic rituals. Using song and dance, the shaman can call the god or evil spirit desired, so that the shaman may act as a spokesperson of the god or evil spirit through hallucination. In traditional Korean society, the music for the shamanic ritual to expel evil spirits has been called Sinawi rhythm. Sinawi rhythm is also called Salpuri rhythm because it is used as the accompaniment of Salpuri-Gut.

There are mainly two arguments about the origin of the word Sinawi. The first claims it originated from *Hyangga*(鄉歌: old Korean folk song) in the kingdom of Silla.[34] The word *Hyang* means "country," and *Ga* means "song." One of the typical folk songs in that time was *Sanoega*(詞腦歌). *Sa* means "poem," and *Noe*, "brain" or "spirit"; therefore, it can be interpreted as the song of a poem reflecting our spirit. This, as folk music, is different from the court music of that period.

The other argument claims the word Sinawi originated from words related to "god," whose Korean pronunciation is "Sin." Thus, some argue that the word originated from the Chinese word, *Sinak*(神樂). *Sin* means god, and *Ak* means music; therefore, Sinak means the music of god. In fact, the pronunciation of Sinak is similar to that of Sinawi.

However, Ji Young-Hi (1909–1979), one of the famous players of the Haegeum, a kind of fiddle, argues that the word was derived from the Chinese word *Sinawi*(神娥慰). *Sin* means god; *A* means "beautiful woman"; and *Wi*, "solace."[35] The beautiful woman refers to the female shaman. Sinawi rhythm is also called *Simbang-Gok*. *Simbang* means "shaman" or "shamanism" in Jeju island, which is located in the south of the Korean peninsula. *Gok* means "rhythm." It is generally said that the Korean word *Simbang* is originated from the Chinese word *Sinbang*(神房). *Bang* means "room"; therefore, Sinbang means the "room of god."

Various traditional musical instruments have been used in Sinawi rhythm. They are *Piri*, a kind of fife or flute; *Daegeum*, a kind of large fife; *Haegeum*, a kind of fiddle; *Jangku*, an hourglass-shaped drum; *Buk*, a kind of drum; *Jing*, a kind of gong made from brass; *Ajaeng*, a wide zither with seven strings made of twisted silk; *Geomungo*, a Korean harp with six strings; and *Gayakum*, a Korean harp with twelve strings. In some cases, *Gueum*(口音: "vocal sound") and *Bara*, similar to a set of cymbals, are added. Sinawi music then is comparable to a small orchestra (see Photo 3). Although varied, each of these instruments produces a somewhat sorrowful sound.

The musical instruments used in Sinawi rhythm are called *Samhyunyookgak*(三絃六角: "three strings and six horns"). Therefore, some people may suppose that the musical instruments consist of three stringed instruments, plus six instruments in the family of wind instruments. However, the reason why Sinawi rhythm is called Samhyunyookgak has not been clearly explained yet. It means just a basic set of musical instruments for playing traditional Korean folk music. Under the accompaniment of Samhyunyookgak, the shaman performs incantations and directs all body movements.

Unlike Korean court music, Sinawi music has no law of harmony, and does not use sheet music. Indeed, it has no regular measure of musical timing. Sinawi music lacks the concept of the metronome as used in western music theory. For example, in Sinawi music, the time interval between beats can be one, two, three, four, five seconds, or more. The interval can be reduced or extended according to the lead player, who is generally playing Jangku. The lead player in Sinawi rhythm adjusts the tempo of the beat by adapting to the shaman's incantations and movements. The shaman essentially takes on the function of a conductor of the Sinawi accompaniment. Thus, Sinawi music is improvisatorial.

The improvisatorial element arises from the Korean people's attitude towards Heung which was explained earlier. Heung is also expressed as *Sinbaram*. The pronunciation of Sin is same as that of the letter referring to god in the Korean language. Baram means "wind." Thus we may say that Sinbaram means "wind of god," although it is not clear whether this letter "Sin" originated in the letter meaning god.

A god does not exist in reality. It exists in our hallucination. We may feel merriment in the hallucination through the role of the ego ideal as pointed out earlier. If so, we can also interpret Sinbaram as the energy to maximize our merriment. Indeed, the Korean people traditionally have been called a "Nation of Heung." Heung or Sinbaram can provide the Korean people with an opportunity to solve their Hahn through their own creative ways. If there is no Sinbaram, the Korean people may not overcome their Hahn. In this sense, Heung or Sinbaram is a manifestation of the Korean people's unconscious to resolve their Hahn.

As mentioned earlier, the Korean people like the number three. Accordingly, each musical beat is divided into three short beats such as "wo-wo-won." This division can provide a certain metronomic quality to the music, although it still lacks the regular measured timing of other types of music. In fact, the three-split-beat system is very important in understanding the essence of Korean traditional music, especially Sinawi rhythm.

There are some different styles of Sinawi rhythms, according to the region. The main difference derives from whether the rhythm is based on a major system or a minor system. In this context, the difference is broadly classified into two types: one is *Gyeonggi*(京畿) style, and the other *Honam*(湖南) style. Gyeonggi is the name of the region located in the west side of the middle Korean peninsula. For example, the city of Seoul is typical of the region of Gyeonggi, whereas Honam is in the southwestern region of the Korean peninsula.

In general, Gyeonggi style evokes a relatively light feeling because it is based on the major rhythm system. Thus, this rhythm may evoke some feelings related to the Korean people's Heung, although Sinawi rhythm focuses on representing the Korean people's Hahn. But the rhythm patterns of Honam style are somewhat different from those of Gyeonggi style. We call the rhythm of the former *Gyemyunjo*(界面調). This rhythm is very feminine, soft, piteous, melancholy, or sorrowful. *Gye* means "a line to decide a certain boundary," *Myun* means "face," and *Jo* means "rhythm." According to the Encyclopedia of Koran National Culture, it is named so because some traces (like lines) of tears appear on our face when we hear the rhythm of Gyemyunjo.[36] In this sense, we can say that Gyemyunjo is based on the minor rhythm.

NOTES

1. Edward B. Tylor, *Primitive Culture: Researches into the Development of Mythology, Philosophy, Religion, Language, Art, and Custom* (New York: G. P. Putnam's Sons, 1920), quoted in Min-Ho Kook, "After-Life of Confucianism Viewed from the Ghost Belief and Ancestral Rites(귀신신앙과 제사를 통해 살펴본 유교의 내세관)," *Society and Theory*(사회와 이론) (Seoul: Association of Korean Social Theory) 7 (2005), 95.
2. Michael Loewe, *Chinese Ideas of Life and Death: Faith, Myth, and Reason in the Han Period (202 BC–AD 220)*, trans. Sung-Kyoo Lee (London: George Allen & Unwin, 1982), 42.
3. Soo-Chung Kim, "A Study of Life, Death, and Ghost in Confucianism," *Sukdangnonchong*(石堂論叢) (Busan, Korea: Sukdang Haksulwon, Dong-A University) 33 (2003): 171–72; see *Sunglidaejeon*(性理大全), ed. Bokyung-Munhwasa (Seoul: Bokyung-Munhwasa, 1994).
4. Yong-Joo Lee, "Ghost, a Repressed Desire from Others(타자의 억물린 욕망)," *Tradition and the Present* (Seoul, Jeontong and Hyundae), 18 (Winter 2001): 38–39.
5. Sigmund Freud, *Totem and Taboo*, trans. James Strachey (New York: W.W. Norton, 1950), 141.
6. Patrick McNamara, *Spirit Possession and Exorcism: History, Psychology, and Neurobiology* (Santa Barbara, CA: Praeger, 2011), 2:36.
7. Freud, *Totem and Taboo*, 59.
8. Ibid., 65.
9. This study is also used to find a good place to live. This theory is called *Yang-Tack* (*Yang* is pronounced the same as in Chinese, and means "positive"; *Tack* means "house"). The study to find a good place for burying is called the theory of *Eum-Tack* (*Yin* in Chinese means "negative" in English).
10. Yong-Shin Kim, *Psychology Meets Korean People*, 121–22.
11. Fred Alford, *Korean Values in the Age of Globalization*, trans. Kyung-Tae Nam (Seoul: Greenbee, 2000), 134. This poem was re-translated into English by Yong-Shin Kim, from Kyung-Tae Nam's Korean translation of the English edition. Also see Ko Un, *The Sound of My Waves* (Seoul: Nanam, 1996).
12. Kwang-Iel Kim, "Shamanism and Personality in Korea," *The Modern Meaning of Shamanism*, ed. Folklore Research Institute (Korea: Won Kwang University, 1972), 89.
13. Neung-Hwa Lee, *Study of the Chosun Shamanism* (Seoul: Association of Korean Culture and Anthropology, 1968), 44.
14. G. J. Ramstedt, *Studies in Korean Etymology*, ed. Pentti Aalto (Helsinki: Suomalaisugrilainen seura, 1953), quoted in Dong-Sik Yoo, *History and Structure of the Korean Shamanism* (Seoul: Yonsei University Press, 1978), 292.
15. *Great Korean Dictionary*, s.v. "굿" (Gut).
16. Heung-Yoon Cho, *The Korean Shamans* (Seoul: Jungeumsa, 1983), 94–111.
17. Byung-Ok Lee, *History of Korean Dance*, 23.
18. *Encyclopedia of Korean Culture*, s.v. "박수무당" (Barksoo-Mudang), accessed October 19, 2016, http://100.daum.net/encyclopedia/view/14XXE0020830.
19. Gil-Sung Choi, *Study of the Korean Shamanism* (Seoul: Asia Munwhasa, 1978), 36–38.
20. *Encyclopedia*(다음백과), s.v. "당골" (Dangol), accessed October 19, 2016, http://100.daum.net/encyclopedia/view/b04d2395a.
21. Max Weber, *On Charisma and Institution Building* (Chicago: University of Chicago Press, 1968), 254.
22. Gil-Sung Choi, *Korean Shamanism*, 184–94.
23. Dong-Sik Yoo, *History of Korean Shamanism*, 314–20.

24. Eun-Joo Lee, "An Analysis of Salpuri-Chum's Structure" (PhD diss., Sejong University, 1997), 37.
25. Gil-Sung Choi, *Korean Shamanism*, 274–78.
26. Byung-Ok Lee, *The Salpuri-Chum: A Study of Its Styles and Lineage*(살풀이춤: 유파와 계통연구) (Seoul: Nori(노리), 2008), 7.
27. Gil-Sung Choi, *Korean Shamanism*, 282–85.
28. Ibid., 8.
29. *Navercast*, s.v. "유치환" (Yoo Chi-Hwan), by Chang Suck-Joo, accessed October 19, 2016, http:// navercast.naver.com/contents.nhn?rid=123&contents_id=7472. The poem "Flag" (깃발) was translated by Yong-Shin Kim.
30. Eun-Joo Lee, *Salpuri-Chum's Structure*, 38.
31. Myung-Hee Han, *Our Rhythm and Our Culture* (Seoul: Chosun Ilbo, 1994), 30–33.
32. Ibid., 83–87.
33. Ibid., 74–77.
34. Tae-Hyun Choi, "Musical Condition of Sinawi and Its Background," *Journal of the Society for Korean Historico-Musicology* (Seoul: The Society for Korean Historico-Musicology) 35 (December 2005): 119–124.
35. EBS's *Sensation* [Korean television program] featured a recorded explanation by Ji Young-Hi of the meaning of "Sinawi(神娥慰)," broadcast Oct. 8, 2012.
36. *Encyclopedia of Korean Culture*, s.v. "계면조" (Gyemyunjo), accessed October 19, 2016, http://terms.naver.com/entry.nhn?docId=567044&cid=46661&categoryId=46661.

Chapter Four

The Development of Salpuri-Chum

GWANGDAE-CHUM AND GISANG-CHUM

Shamanic rituals including songs and dances had strongly influenced popular entertainment in Korean society. In the Confucian society, popular entertainers belonged to the lowest class; however, most people, including even the people in the highest class, enjoyed seeing their performances. This is ironic because the higher class always emphasized morality, which prevented the direct expression of desire.

Confucius, like Socrates and Plato, viewed the human being as having two main elements, *Li*(理: "reason") and *Ki*(氣: "desire"; the Chinese pronunciation is "Chi").[1] Simply speaking, Li is related to spirit, and Ki to the body. For Confucius, a human being can be a civilized being only when Li controls Ki, because he emphasizes a certain social order. In this sense, Confucianism has repressed some emotions related to the pleasure of the body. This is the reason that the popular entertainers' direct representations of their emotions could not be recognized as noble behavior. Despite this, most people, including the noble class, enjoyed the performances of popular entertainers, because they also felt a catharsis from their performances.

In the Korean traditional society, popular entertainers were called *Gwangdae*(廣大). The Chinese letter *Gwang* means "wide," and *Dae*, "big." However, most Korean people have understood the word as a masque performer, a puppeteer, or an acrobat performer; therefore, the performances included music, song, and dance. Unfortunately, there is no study which clearly explains the reason why the Chinese letters are used for explaining popular entertainers.

Of course, there are other words referring to popular entertainers in the traditional society. Among them, two words are more common than the others. These are *Changwoo*(倡優) and *Jaein*(才人). The letter *Chang* means "singer" or "professional entertainer," and *Woo*, "actor" or "professional entertainer." In addition, the letter *Jae* means "talent," and *In*, "person." These names are more understandable than Gwangdae. However, Gwangdae is more popular than any other word when we refer to popular entertainers in the traditional society.

The history of Gwangdae is very long. According to the dictionary, the word Gwangdae, meaning a popular entertainer who sang various songs with a mask, appeared in some historical records from the kingdom of Koryeo.[2] Several Gwangdaes played together at various performances including singing, dancing, acrobatics, and so forth. They also sometimes participated in some shamanic rituals, especially the various Guts. For example, they sang and danced as the assistants of the shaman directing the Gut.

In the Chosun dynasty, the activities of Gwangdae were more widely spread out than in the Kingdom of Koryeo. In this era, some local governments organized the official associations of Gwangdae called *Jaeincheong*(才人廳). *Jaein* means "Gwangdae," as mentioned earlier, and *Cheong* means "office." Records show that Gwangdaes tried to establish a national association in Seoul in 1824.[3]

Gwangdaes did not exhibit their talents alone; they always conducted their performances as a group. Most of the Gwangdaes were males. Those belonging to Jaeincheong usually participated in Guts, and they performed their own programs in their own regions. However, they came to Seoul to conduct their performances when there were some national events, such as receptions for foreign envoys, and ceremonies for people who passed governmental examinations.

The various groups of Gwangdae performed their artistic activities while wandering from place to place. In fact, the shaman's movements were relatively simple and repetitious. But shamanic movements developed as they were taken up by groups of Gwangdae, especially in the Chosun dynasty. Despite the fact that Gwangdae held a very low social status even in the Chosun dynasty, the activities of Gwangdae had a strong influence on Korean music and dance. As this development continued over time, the shaman's simple and repeated movements became increasingly sophisticated as they adapted to Sinawi rhythm.

As a result, some groups of Gwangdae created their own special performances, such as masque dance, rope dancing, and "play in yard" (*Madang-nori*:마당놀이). Most of their programs were very humorous, and sometimes satirical. Through their performances, the people exhaled their Heung and sometimes felt a certain catharsis. Some of the programs created by the Gwangdae group are recognized today as very important national or local cultural treasures.

The traditional Confucian society was very authoritarian. Thus, it was very difficult for ordinary people to express their feelings toward the upper class. However, Gwangdae, using various masks symbolizing the different classes, represented the discontents of the lower class with satirical characterizations. Thus, an entertainer having the mask symbolizing the higher class could be disgraced by the entertainer having the mask symbolizing the lower class. In this kind of scene, most people felt a catharsis. In the Confucian reality, the lower class could not criticize the higher class; however, it was possible to do this in the Gwangdae's performance. Therefore, the Gwangdae's performance provided the people with the opportunities to enjoy their Heung as well as to pacify their Hahn.

There is another very interesting element to note for understanding the performances by Gwangdae. This element is the peculiarity of the stage for their performance. In Korean traditional society, most stages were on the outside of the building. This meant that the stages were open, and audiences watched the performances of Gwangdae from all sides. The audience formed a circle, and Gwangdaes performed their programs inside the circle. Even in governmental events, the stage was surrounded by the audience. In other words, the stage automatically became a theater-in-the-round. Gwangdaes, therefore, performed their programs while turning around in all directions towards the audience.

The shaman's primitive dance was also adapted by *Gisang*(妓生). *Gi* as a Chinese letter means "female hostess who has some talents," and *Sang*, "birth" or "person." As the letters indicate, Gisang was a female entertainer who acted as a hostess at parties and bars, often referred to as Gisang houses. Gisangs were skilled in the performance of traditional music, dance, and song. In addition to performances, Gisangs were skilled in conversation.

In this sense, Gisang was also called *Hae-Er-Hwa*(解語花), The letter *Hae* means "understanding"; *Er*, "talking"; and *Hwa*, "flower." Thus, the word means "the speaking flower which understands language." The history of Gisang is also very long. According to Lee Neung-Hwa, a Korean historian, Gisang supposedly originated from the *Wonhwa-Jedo* (源or原花 制度) in the early years of the kingdom of Silla.[4] The Wonhwa-Jedo aimed at training young girls for leadership, and it was later changed into the *Hwarang-Jedo*(花郞制度) which trained young boys for national security.

But whether or not Gisangs began to appear in the kingdom of Silla, their role and activities became clearer through the Koryeo-Yeoak(高麗女樂), an organization of talented young girls trained for national events or ceremonies in the kingdom of Koryeo. The word *Yeoak* means "female musician." At that time, there were many female musicians managed by the government. For example, there were about 260 Yeoaks who participated only in ceremonies for the king.[5]

In fact, beginning in the eleventh century in the kingdom of Koryeo, the female entertainers known as Gisang began playing a very active role.[6] Young girls who wanted to become Gisangs entered a professional school, where they learned singing, dancing, playing musical instruments, Korean traditional poetry, Oriental calligraphy, drawing, and more. The educational system for Gisangs was continued in the Chosun dynasty. Thus, Gisangs were treated as well-educated persons although their social status was very low.[7]

The kingdom of Koryeo established *Gyobang*(教坊), which taught Gisang. *Gyo* means "school," and *Bang*, "special house." This points to the Gyobang as a Gisang school using a special house. During this period, a Gyobang controlled the Yeoak, which was mentioned above. Gyobang were continually operated in the Chosun dynasty, and controlled Gisangs belonging to the government. The governmental organization which managed Gyobang was called *Gyobangcheong*(教坊廳); *Cheong* means "governmental office." Also, both concepts are usually used without separating them from each other.

In the Chosun dynasty there were two kinds of Gisangs: one was the private Gisang, and the other was the government Gisang. The latter are called *Gwangi*(官妓). The letter *Gwan* means "government," and *Gi* stood for Gisang. Gwangi danced to the accompaniment of *Jeongak*(正樂: "court music," in Korean), which had a very slow tempo, regular measured timing, and sheet music. Jeongak was used in government rituals and events.

However, most of the private Gisangs, in contrast, followed the dances of shamans and Gwangdae based on Korean folk music. The private Gisangs especially liked to use Sinawi rhythm as the accompaniment of their dances and songs. This was because ordinary people were more familiar with the improvisational or sentimental rhythm based on the Korean people's Heung and Hahn.

When Gisangs expressed merriment (Heung) in their performances, they danced with their scarves, which supposedly originated from the traditional singer's handkerchief. The Korean traditional singers would sometimes shake their handkerchiefs in order to excite the audience, increasing their Heung. More practically, the scarves were also used for wiping the sweat from their faces. Furthermore, when they sang a very sorrowful song, they wiped their tears with their handkerchiefs or scarves. The audiences watching their behavior would also cry together with the performers. For these reasons, the singers would keep their handkerchiefs at the ready, in the sleeves of their Korean traditional dress, which pouched in the middle and could be used as pockets.

When Gisang danced with the scarves, they fluttered them, using them in more sophisticated movements. The use of the scarf was inspired by the long piece of fabric that shamans used in Guts. Therefore, the Gisang dance with

Sinawi rhythm was called the scarf dance (*Soogun-Chum*, in Korean). These dances were performed by private Gisang for the pleasure of the participants. The stages of Gisangs were also round, although the performances were held in a relatively wide room; therefore, unlike Gwangdae, they could not use the full width of the room.

In the case of Gisang-Chum, the limitation of the space rather contributed to the development of the sophisticated movements. In order to dance in a small space, each movement of the dancer had to be more detailed; otherwise, it is difficult to move the audiences' minds. For this reason, the Gisang tried to develop a variety of new movements. In the process, they also developed some new ways to use the handkerchief or scarf to evoke the audiences' Heung or sorrow.

THE ROLE OF HAN SUNG-JUN FOR MODERN SALPURI-CHUM

Korean society changed rapidly in the 20th Century. The Chosun dynasty was finished and the Korean peninsula was, unfortunately, colonized by Japan. From that time, Western culture began flowing into Korean society. In this period of change, the groups of Gwangdae reorganized and their artistic activities were modernized, incorporating parts of western music and dance. Their dance movements became more systematic even as they continued to dance to the improvisational Sinawi rhythm.

With the collapse of the Chosun dynasty, the government-supported system of Gwangi disappeared. Thus, some of the Gwangi became the personally-hired Gisang at private bars; this included the women. The tradition of Gisang in the colonial period was maintained through *Gwonbeon*(券番), schools that taught the basic skills of traditional music, song, and dance. Through Gwonbeon, Gisang began to grow. Indeed, the Japanese government asked Gisangs to organize into an association so the colonial government could control Gisang activity. For Gisangs, the association offered support and opportunities to perform their skills in some stages.[8]

The Gisang's studies of traditional dances, through Gwonbeon and performances in public places, contributed to the development of the movements of Salpuri-Chum based on Sinawi music. These movements became more artistic, with fewer ritualistic elements of shamanic dance. The Gisang dance also changed from a collective dance into a solo dance, because of the smaller space which the Gisang had at private bars compared to the larger governmental halls.[9]

Into this situation came a pioneer in the rearrangement (or standardization) of Gisang and Gwangdae improvisatorial dance for the theatrical Salpuri-Chum. He was Han Sung-Jun(韓成俊: 1874–1941). Although born into a noble family, he became a Gwangdae.[10] His deep knowledge of the essence of Korean traditional music arose from his mastery of the traditional drum, providing him an intimate understanding of rhythm that he brought into Sinawi music and dance. Han declared, "The most important element of all kinds of music is rhythm, and the rhythm is based on dance."[11] Indeed, he argued that every human movement could be sublimated into dance.[12] The dancer can act as conductor to the music.

Han established the Institute of Chosun Music and Dance in 1934, and held his first dance performance at *Bumingwan*(府民館), a theater in Seoul in 1936.[13] In this first performance, he danced *Seung-Mu*(僧舞: "Buddhist dance") and Salpuri-Chum.[14] Indeed, his performances introduced twentieth-century Korea to several Korean traditional dances such as *Taepyung-Mu*(太平舞: "dance of peace"), *Geom-Mu*(劍舞: "sword dance"), and *Hanlyang-Mu*(閑良舞: "dance of a gentleman").

During his lifetime, Han developed many dances for theatrical performance by rearranging the special movements of Gwangdae and Gisang dances, as well as Korean shamanic and court dances. Through this process, he developed about forty repertoires.[15] Although some dances did not succeed, dances such as Seung-Mu, Taepyung-Mu, Geom-Mu, *Hark-Mu*(鶴舞: "crane dance"), and Salpuri-Chum, became national or provincial cultural treasures. In short, he rearranged the various Korean traditional dances performed in the open and round stages, for the dances of the proscenium.

It is said that his first performance of Salpuri-Chum lasted only three minutes. In these three minutes, however, he provided the essential aspects of its form, such as dividing the dance into three parts based upon the speed of the rhythm. It is also said that he wore the Korean traditional men's white clothing, and danced with a piece of white silk fabric. His choice made clear the essential meaning of Salpuri-Chum. In Korean, the color white is associated symbolically with purity, so much so that the Korean people have been historically referred to as the *Baek-Eui-Min-Jok*(白衣民族: "White Clothes Nation").[16] The Chinese letter *Baek* means "white"; *Eui*, "clothes," and *Min-jok*, "nation." This association, symbolically and historically, may have inspired Han's choice.

Han tried to create artistic movements through the harmonious movement of the arms with the scarf and the skirt. Korean traditional dance emphasizes the arms and shoulder. This focus on the movement of the upper body may be because the traditional long skirt for women hides the legs, and thus their movement. At best, the movement of the legs created soft shapes through the long skirt. In this sense, the Korean traditional dance is the antithesis of western ballet, which focuses on the movement of the legs. Han probably arranged the movements of Salpuri-Chum according to shamanistic movements, infusing meaning into each position.

In Salpuri-Chum, the upper body movements have special meaning.[17] For example, lifting the arms up means pleasure, placing the hands on the waist means thinking, joining two hands means mystical union, holding a hand to the neck means sacrifice, and placing a hand on the eye means death. The right hand means reason and reality, while the left hand means the emotions, the unconscious, or the ideal.

Han's Salpuri-Chum later developed into various styles. Among them, three became major styles: Han Young-Sook, Lee Mae-Bang, and Kim Sook-Ja. Variations arose in movements, rhythm, style of clothing, and size of the fabrics used in the dance. However, the basic structure established by Han did not obviously change, even as the time expanded to fifteen minutes.

BASIC STRUCTURE OF SALPURI-CHUM AND ITS MEANING

Salpuri-Chum consists of three parts based on the speed of the Sinawi rhythm. The rhythm of the first part is very slow, the second part is fast, and the third part is slow again. It is an A-B-A rhythm structure. The timing of each part varies. For example, the first part comprises almost two-thirds of the entire performance. If the total performance time of the Salpuri-Chum is fifteen minutes, the first part is ten minutes; the second part is four minutes; and the third part is one minute. This is derived from the main characteristics of Korean music, especially Sinawi rhythm in which the first part is very long.

The stage curtain is not closed when each part is finished; instead, the parts are smoothly connected. The speed of the rhythm of the first part begins slowly, gradually becoming faster, to the point where it changes into the second part. Then the speed of the second part gradually slows, until it changes into the third part.

If we consider the form of Salpuri-Gut, the philosophical meaning of each part in Salpuri-Chum can be interpreted as follows:

The first part has two purposes. The first purpose is to call forth the evil spirit that is causing harm to the living person. The second purpose is to ask the evil spirit its wish. The dance movements for this purpose express solemnity because of the importance of speaking with the evil spirit about its Hahn. The second part's purpose is to resolve the Hahn of the evil spirit. The act of resolving the Hahn is the climax of Salpuri-Chum. The dancer's movements become dynamic as the dancer attempts to convey joy to the evil spirit, so the spirit can experience happiness and find solace, resolving its Hahn. The third part is a farewell. With the Hahn resolved, the evil spirit becomes a soul who then ascends into the highest place in the sky. The dancer's movements display the sublime satisfaction that the soul must be feeling in its ascendance.

The rhythm structure of Salpuri-Chum also provides insight into the nature of Salpuri-Chum. The steps in Salpuri-Chum rhythm structure have historical antecedents in traditional folk music. Oh Sung-Sam (1866–1936), a famous traditional drummer, and Kim Yeon-Soo (1907–1974), a famous Korean traditional singer, are credited with the development of the traditional dance steps into Salpuri-Chum steps.[18] These developments progressed with the adaptation of Oh's drumming style, and with Kim's application of Chinese poetic structure.[19]

The rhythm structure has four steps. They are called *Gi*(起), *Gyeong*(輕), *Gyeol*(結), and *Hae*(解) in Chinese. Gi means "the beginning"; Gyeong, "development"; Gyeol, "climax" (peak or tension); and Hae, "solution" (relax or relieve). The Korean equivalents for these movements are *Milgo* (pushing), *Dalgo* (connecting), *Maetgo* (tensioning), and *Pulgo* (relieving). The Korean traditional music perceives a need for relaxation of the rhythm after the climax. As such, Korean traditional music adds the concept of Hae after Gyeol onto the structure of Chinese poetry. Chinese poetry has four steps in developing and concluding its form: *Gi*(起), *Seung*(承), *Jeon*(轉), and *Gyeol*(結). Gi means "starting" (arousing); Seung, "developing"; Jeon, "changing" or "converting"; and Gyeol, "concluding." In Korean traditional music, to maintain the four-step structure with the addition of Hae, Seung and Jeon are combined into Gyeong.

A Korean musician who studies traditional music says, "Our rhythm has the structure of Gi, Gyeong, Gyeol, and Hae. Every theory begins, develops and concludes. It is also natural to start again after relieving tension. In this process, the most important part is to relieve tension."[20] This reflects the belief that an ending provokes tension, and therefore that tension must be relieved. In this context, Salpuri-Chum frames the four steps as follows: the first part contains Gi and Gyeong; the second part brings Gyeol; and the third part is Hae.

NOTES

1. Yong-Shin Kim, *Ki Dae-Seung, a Korean Theorist of Human Nature, meets Freud* (Seoul: Yemunseowon, 2002), 20–36.
2. *Dictionary of Korean Traditional Entertainment*(한국전통연희사전), s.v. "광대" (Kwangdae), ed. Minsokwon Publishing (http://www.minsokwon.com/), accessed October 19, 2016, http://terms.naver.com/entry.nhn?docId=3325665&cid=56785&categoryId=56785.
3. Ibid.
4. Neung-Hwa Lee, *A History of Hae-Er-Hwa in the Chosun Dynasty* (Seoul: Dongmunsun, 1992), 19.
5. *Encyclopedia of Korean Culture*, s.v. "여악" (Yeoak), accessed October 19, 2016, http://terms.naver.com/entry.nhn?docId=795214&cid=46666&categoryId=46666.
6. Byung-Ok Lee, *Salpuri-Chum: Styles and Lineage*, 33.
7. Ibid., 34.
8. Kyung-Ae Kim, Chae-Hyun Kim, and Jong-Ho Lee, *The Hundred Years of Our Dance* (Seoul: Hyunamsa, 2001), 24.
9. Ibid., 37.
10. Eun-Joo Lee, *The Thirty Three Dancers* (Seoul: Pureun Media, 2007), 11.

11. "Han Sung-Jun as a Drummer for 50 Years(鼓手 五十年 韓成俊氏)," *Chosun Ilbo* (Seoul), March 27, 1937.

12. "The Sublimation of Classical Arts(古典藝術의 一大精華)," *Chosun Ilbo* (Seoul), November 8, 1939.

13. Byung-Ok Lee, *Salpuri-Chum: Styles and Lineage*, 39; Mal-Bok Kim, *The Understanding of Dance* (Seoul: Yejeonsa, 1999), 361. Kim argues in this book that Han organized the Institute of Chosun Music and Dance in 1930; Il-Ji Moon, *The Heart to Protect Dance* (Seoul: Korean Dance Academy, 1969), 42–47. According to this author, the first dance performance of Han Sung-Jun was held at Bumingwan (a Theater in Seoul) in 1935. The first newspaper record of the performance of Salpuri-Chum at Bumingwan appeared in *Chosun Ilbo* (Seoul), June 19, 1938.

14. Il-Ji Moon, *Heart to Protect*, 44–45.

15. Kyung-Ae Kim, Chae-Hyun Kim, and Jong-Ho Lee, *The Hundred Years*, 39–40.

16. *Encyclopedia of Korean Culture*, s.v. "백의민족" (Baek-Eui-Min-Jok), accessed October 27, 2016, http://terms.naver.com/entry.nhn?docId=557162&cid=46634&categoryId=46634.

17. Byung-Ok Lee, *Salpuri-Chum: Styles and Lineage,* 79; Kyu-Hee Kim, "The 'Hahn' Presented in the Salpuri-Chum," (master's thesis, Wonkwang University, 1996) 17–18. In this study, the Hahn means a regrettable feeling or mourning of the Korean people.

18. Bo-Hyung Lee, "A Comparative Study of the Generation between Dalgo-Maekki and Gi-Gyeong-Gyeol-Hae: Focused on the Meaning Indicated by the Rhythmic Patterns of Jungjungmori and Jinyang," in *Studies in Korean Music* (Seoul: Korean Musicological Society) no. 39 (2006), 223.

19. Ibid., 224.

20. "Park Bum-Hoon: The Need of Chuimsae in Heartless Society(박범훈: 각박한 사회에 '추임새' 절실), *Kyunghyang Sinmun* (Seoul), October 22, 2008.

Photo 1: Gopuri Performance.

Photo 2: Gilgareum Performance.

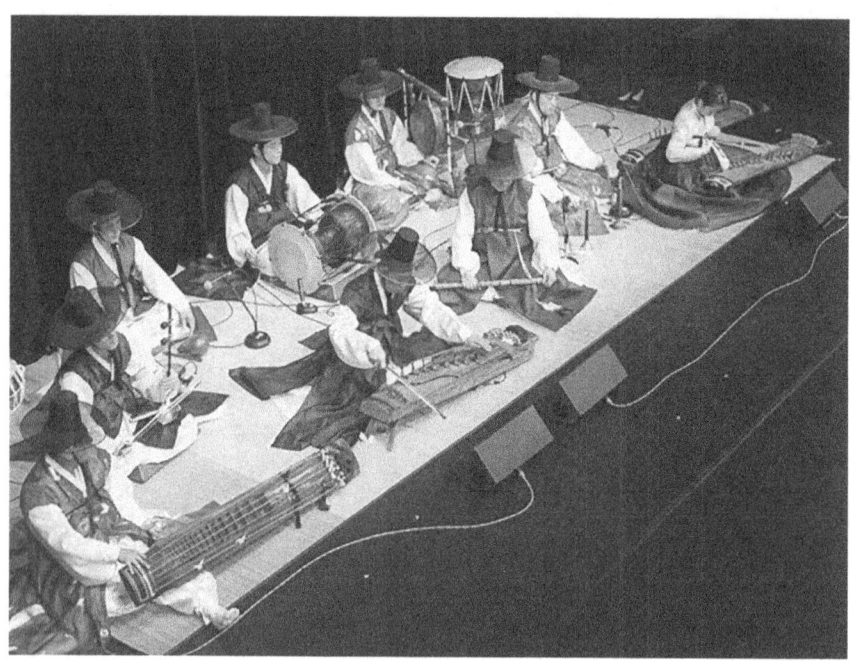

Photo 3: Sinawi Accompaniment.

Photo 4: Han Young-Sook's Salpuri-Chum.

Photo 5: Han Young-Sook's Salpuri-Chum.

Photo 6: Han Young-Sook's Salpuri-Chum.

Photo 7: Lee Mae-Bang's Salpuri-Chum.

Photo 8: Lee Mae-Bang's Salpuri-Chum.

Photo 9: Lee Mae-Bang's Salpuri-Chum.

Photo 10: Kim Sook-Ja's Dosalpuri-Chum.

Photo 11: Kim Sook-Ja's Dosalpuri-Chum.

Photo 12: Kim Sook-Ja's Dosalpuri-Chum.

Photo 13: Kwon Myung-Hwa's Salpuri-Chum.

Photo 14: Kwon Myung-Hwa's Salpuri-Chum.

Photo 15: Choi Sun's Salpuri-Chum.

Photo 16: Choi Sun's Salpuri-Chum.

Photo 17: Kim Bok-Ryun's Salpuri-Chum.

Photo 18: Kim Bok-Ryun's Salpuri-Chum.

Photo 19: Kim Ran's Salpuri-Chum.

Photo 20: Kim Ran's Salpuri-Chum.

Photo 21: Lee Eun-Joo's Salpuri-Chum.

Photo 22: Lee Eun-Joo's Salpuri-Chum.

Photo 23: Lee Eun-Joo's Salpuri-Chum.

Photo 24: Lee Eun-Joo's Salpuri-Chum.

Photo 25: Lee Eun-Joo's Salpuri-Chum.

Photo 26: Lee Eun-Joo's Salpuri-Chum.

Chapter Five

Three Main Styles of Salpuri-Chum

HAN YOUNG-SOOK STYLE

Han Young-Sook(韓英淑: 1920–1989) is a granddaughter of Han Sung-Jun. She started to learn Korean traditional dance from her grandfather when she was thirteen years old.[1] When she was eighteen years old, she had her first Salpuri-Chum performance in Bumingwan, where her grandfather first performed his dances. Her grandfather declared her his successor due to the pride he felt in her abilities.[2]

After her grandfather died, she managed the Institute of Chosun Music and Dance that he had established. She became a professor in the Department of Dance in Soodo(首都) Women Teachers College (currently Sejong University:世宗大學校) in 1974. She performed her Salpuri-Chum in the final ceremony of Seoul Olympic Games in 1988, showing the essence of the Korean traditional dance to the world.

For her style, she adapted her grandfather's Salpuri-Chum by expanding the performance time from ten to fifteen minutes. This can be regarded as a very important work to develop Salpuri-Chum as a perfect theatrical dance in the present time. She extended or reduced the time of the performance according to the situation. Of course, the basic three structures of the dance are also adjusted according to the performance time. Most dancers who wanted to perform Salpuri-Chum later followed the time which she had developed.

At first, she wore the traditional women's blue-colored skirt and white jacket in her performances. Later, she consciously changed the clothes to the white jacket and skirt, as well as a piece of white silk fabric, to symbolize that purity is at the core of Korean culture. The white silk fabric was considered vital to Salpuri-Chum; and according to Lee Eun-Joo, a student of Han Young-Sook, the proper length is about ten centimeters longer than the dancer's height, with the width being the same as a piece of fabric woven on a traditional loom.³ That makes its length about 1.7 to 1.8 meters, and its width about forty-five centimeters.

Han used the arms and shoulder more than the legs. Indeed, there are no leaps. Steps are taken by lifting the legs slowly, keeping them hidden in the long skirt. This gave her steps a smooth and gentle appearance. On the stage, she moves first to the right; second, to the left; third, to the front; and, fourth, around the stage.

She keeps her movements temperate, giving them a stable and noble bearing. Because of this, her movements have sometimes been interpreted as masculine. This quality might be due to her learning the dance from her grandfather. She also flutters the white silk fabric naturally, moving it without a plan. These aspects make her dance straightforward, without extraneous complexity that might confuse the essence for the audience.

Han uses the three-split-beat for her accompaniment, with twelve short beats in a bar that contains four main beats. This is typical of Sinawi rhythm, and one that she inherited from her grandfather. Her grandfather traveled the country, combining the characteristics of various local Sinawi rhythms into the model for theatrical Salpuri-Chum. This Salpuri-Chum is called the moderate form, because it mixes the various local dances. Han's style developed from this moderate form; it is said to represent the core characteristics of Sinawi rhythm, especially in the Seoul area belonging to the Gyeonggi region, where she spent most of her life. In this sense, we can call her style the Seoul Salpuri-Chum.

The major rhythm structure of Han's style may appear to be most conducive to evoking light feelings. Yet the movements, noble and temperate in form, are capable of conveying darker tones, such as the mourning of the Korean people.⁴ This dichotomy of movement and accompaniment can be seen in her work based on the major rhythm (see Photos 4, 5, and 6).

Salpuri-Chum was recognized as an intangible cultural treasure (No. 97) by the government in 1990. Unfortunately, Han died in 1989; therefore, she cannot be recognized as a living human treasure in the field of Salpuri-Chum. But, by her efforts she founded a new era for Salpuri-Chum as a theatrical dance, and strongly influenced other styles. Indeed, her style continues to be taught as an important form of Salpuri-Chum.

LEE MAE-BANG STYLE

Lee Mae-Bang(李梅芳: 1927–2015) was born in the southwestern region of the Korean peninsula. He first learned traditional dance from his grandfather, who was a famous traditional dancer in his region. He studied various traditional dances at a Gwonbeon from seven years of age.⁵ He went to Manchuria in 1939 for middle school, and during this period he became apprenticed to Bae Goo-Ja, a famous traditional dancer.[6]

Upon returning to Korea, he participated in numerous theatrical performances and tried developing his own style of Salpuri-Chum. This attempt was based on Han Sung-Jun's efforts, although he did not directly learn from Han. His dancing talent was first recognized in his performance at the Seoul YMCA auditorium in 1977.[7]

In his performances, Lee wore a man's traditional white ensemble, including a man's traditional long gown, *Kwaeja*. He also wore a *Nambawoo*, which is actually a woman's winter hat. He probably used the hat to symbolize the feminine. Indeed, Kwaeja could be used to mimic the movement of a woman's traditional skirt in Salpuri-Chum. He also used a piece of white silk fabric that was a little shorter than that used by Han Young-Sook. It was about 1.5 meters long and fifty centimeters wide.[8] The shorter length potentially made its movements more elaborate.

Indeed, Salpuri-Chum is generally seen as a woman's dance, because shamans, from whose dances Salpuri-Chum originates, were mostly women; and, as noted earlier, the concept of Hahn closely aligns with the plight of women at the time in Korea. The feminine associations of the dance did not inhibit Lee from performing Salpuri-Chum, probably because Han Sung-Jun first developed it into a theatrical dance.

Lee, unlike Han Young-Sook, focused his movements on steps, making his legs more active than his arms and shoulders. His steps are relatively short, emphasizing the rapid movement of his legs when moving on stage. The rapid leg movements mean that his movements must be nimble and delicate. The focus on leg movements may result from the fact that, lacking a woman's skirt, the motion of his legs were not hidden; therefore, he had to actively incorporate them into the dance.

Lee would display the feminine characteristics of the dance through twisting his body and other techniques, including fluttering the white fabric into a variety of shapes. The rapid, nimble leg movements combined with the twisting of his body made his dance very technical and feminine (see Photos 7, 8, and 9). Indeed, Lee would always present his body in an oblique stance so that the audiences could see his movements from any direction.

The Sinawi accompaniment for Lee's Salpuri-Chum originated from the shamanic ritual in the Honam region, which is in the southwestern region of the Korean peninsula. This rhythm is called Gyemyunjo and is based on a sorrowful minor rhythm, differentiating it from the light major rhythm of Han Young-Sook, and provoking dynamic feelings as solace to mourning.

Lee became a living human treasure when Salpuri-Chum was recognized as a cultural treasure by the government in 1990. His style is seen as an important form of Salpuri-Chum, and he continues to strongly influence the field of Korean traditional dance. Many dances now study his style of Salpuri-Chum.

Unfortunately, he died in 2015. So far, no one has succeeded to his title as a living human cultural treasure. Regarding the recognition of the living human cultural treasures in the field of Salpuri-Chum, a more detailed explanation will be forthcoming, when we discuss the current situation of Salpuri-Chum.

KIM SOOK-JA STYLE

Kim Sook-Ja(金淑子: 1927–1991) was born into a shamanic family. Her mother was a hereditary shaman, and one of her mother's nephews was a famous shamanic musician.[9] Her grandfather was also a famous traditional singer in his region, and her father was a dancer. Thus, she was very familiar with shamanic rituals including traditional music and dance. She began to learn the traditional dances from her father, becoming well known as a traditional dancer by the age of fourteen. At twenty-nine years of age, she operated her own dance school in the city of Daejeon(大田), in the midwest area of South Korea; she managed it for twelve years and taught the various types of traditional dances.[10]

Kim had danced shamanic dances since the early 1970s; though she was influenced partly by Han Sung-Jun, she developed her own style of Salpuri-Chum, *Dosalpuri-Chum*, on the basis of the *Dodang-Gut* in Gyeonggi province, near Seoul. *Dodang*(都堂) means "the village house"; and the Dodang-Gut is a shamanic ritual performed in the village house, where the shaman prays for prosperity and peace for the village.[11]

Thus Dodang-Gut, focused on village prosperity, is different from Salpuri-Gut, which centers on individual happiness. Irrespective of the substantive differences, the basic structural form of Dodang-Gut remains similar to Salpuri-Gut; that is, the shaman, through this Gut, asks the god to expel an evil spirit. Because of this distinction in her Salpuri-Chum from other styles, Kim, along with Lee Mae-Bang, became a living human treasure in the field of Salpuri-Chum in 1990.

Kim wears a woman's traditional white clothes. The style of her clothes is more humble than that of Han Young-Sook; she also ties a piece of white fabric about the waist in the style of a female shaman. She dances with a long piece of white silk fabric about three meters in length, similar in length to those used in shamanic rituals, and fifty centimeters in width.[12]

Kim places the long piece of white fabric around her shoulder as she dances, sometimes fluttering the fabric strongly by moving her knee and waist. For this movement, her steps are relatively wide and her upper body moves actively.[13] To increase the fluttering of the fabric, Kim sometimes ties her long skirt with a fabric belt.

Kim uses the full stage to take advantage of her extensive movements. These wide movements, which reflect many shamanic movements, make her Salpuri-Chum very solemn and grand. There is an earnest sense of ritual in this Salpuri-Chum, especially as Kim tries to make symbolic shapes related to shamanic rituals with the fluttering long white fabric. When she is fluttering the long white fabric, and has the long skirt tightened by a white fabric belt, we feel as if all evil spirits have been expelled (see Photos 10, 11, and 12).

Kim uses the so-called Dosalpuri rhythm, a kind of Sinawi rhythm. However, it is a little different from the other Salpuri rhythms. The Dosalpuri rhythm takes six main beats in a bar, and each main beat is split into two short beats.[14] Two short beats in six main beats may seem the same as three short beats in four main beats, because they both consist of the total twelve short beats in a bar; but the two short beats rhythm is very dynamic.

The movements based on two short beats in a main beat are more active than those based on three short beats in a main beat. This rhythm also coordinates the dance movements with the dancer's breathing. While this rhythm is based on the minor, the movements based on the two-split-beats counterpoints the active rhythm with a sorrowful feeling. As such, Kim Sook-Ja's Salpuri-Chum is different from the others in the rhythm.

Unfortunately, Kim died in 1991; thus, her style did not become widespread, although some dancers tried to study her style. Another reason her style did not become wide-spread is because of her style's close association with Dodang-Gut and shamanic rituals. Moreover, few people are able to play the Dosalpuri rhythm. Despite this, her style is recognized as an important form of Salpuri-Chum, which needs to be protected for the artistic variety of Salpuri-Chum.

NOTES

1. Il-Ji Moon, *Heart to Protect*, 34.
2. Eun-Joo Lee, *Thirty Three Dancers*, 59.
3. This is based on the personal recollections of Lee Eun-Joo of information from her dance teacher, Han Young-Sook.
4. Eun-Joo Lee, *Thirty Three Dancers*, 61.
5. Gyu-Won Lee, *The Hundred Korean Traditional Artists* (Seoul: Hyunamsa, 1995), 430.
6. Byung-Ok Lee, *Salpuri-Chum: Styles and Lineage*, 59.
7. Ibid.; also see Bum-Tae Chung, *Dance and the Dancers* (Seoul: Yeolhwadang, 1992).
8. Byung-Ok Lee, *Salpuri-Chum: Styles and Lineage*, 81.
9. Gyu-Won Lee, *Korean Traditional Artists*, 430.
10. Ibid., 64.
11. *Great Korean Dictionary*, s.v. "도당" (Dodang).
12. Gyu-Won Lee, *Korean Traditional Artists*, 402.
13. Eun-Joo Lee, *Thirty Three Dancers*, 94.
14. Byung-Ok Lee, *Salpuri-Chum: Styles and Lineage*, 69.

Chapter Six

Other Styles of Salpuri-Chum as Local Cultural Treasures

KWON MYUNG-HWA STYLE

Kwon Myung-Hwa(權明花: 1934–) was born in Gyeong-Buk(慶北) province, located in the east side of the Korean peninsula. Her father and grandfather were Barksoo. Her mother helped her father's shamanic works, although she was not Mudang. She suffered twice from Sin-Byung; however, she never allowed herself to become a Mudang, and used various remedies to overcome the Sin-Byung.[1] She really hated her parents' shamanic work.

She had a talent for singing and dancing. When she was only fourteen years old, she decided to go to a Gwonbeon (*Daedong Gwonbeon*) in the city of Daegu(大邱) in the eastern Korean peninsula, and began to learn traditional dance from Park Ji-Hong(박지홍), a famous dancer at that time. Park's hometown was in Honam region. He learned Korean traditional music and dance from Park Gi-Hong(박기홍), whose hometown was the same as his own.[2] The two Parks both acted in the Gwonbeon in the city of Mokpo(木浦), located in Honam; and they both moved to Daegu in the 1940s. Their dancing style was therefore based on the traditional music of Honam, especially Honam Sinawi rhythm.

According to Lee Eun-Joo's study, Kwon's career can be summarized as follows:[3]

Kwon became an adopted daughter of Park Ji-Hong, and had worked as a trainer in the Park Ji-Hong Dance School in Daegu since 1955. After Park's death, she opened her own dancing school in Seoul in 1963; however, in 1964 she returned to Daegu and opened her own dancing school there. In 1965, she received the prize of the Governor of Gyeong-Buk Province in the Fifth National Folklore Contest; and in 1966 she presented a solo theatrical dancing performance. She finally became the living human cultural treasure of Daegu Metropolitan City(大邱廣域市) in the field of Salpuri-Chum (No. 9), in 1995.

The style of Kwon's Salpuri-Chum is said to be based on that of Park Ji-Hong. Park's style has the same root as Lee Mae-Bang Style, because both are based on the Honam Sinawi rhythm called Gyemyunjo. However, there are some differences between them; and Kwon developed her teacher's style.

The most important characteristic of Kwon's Salpuri-Chum is performance of the Gopuri in her dance. She uses a long white silk fabric (1.5 meters long, and fifty centimeters wide) like other dancers; but she ties and unties the fabric in order to recall the Gopuri-Gut explained earlier. She also sometimes twines and untwines the long fabric around her body. Of course, she wears the traditional white clothing, like other dancers; however, her presentation with the fabric gives us a different feeling.

The steps of Lee Mae-Bang are nimble, even though he uses the very sorrowful rhythm of Gyemyunjo. However, Kwon's steps are very wide and relatively slow; thus her steps are manly. This is another difference from the style of Lee Mae-Bang. She hesitates to bend her back, but twirls and rotates about the stage. She also sometimes lifts her knees high, and when walking on the stage mainly uses the back of her foot rather than the front.

Thus Kwon's movements are rough and relatively blunt, compared with those of Lee Mae-Bang. From this view, a study of Kwon's style (see Photos 13 and 14) comments that it represents the typical characteristics of the people in the Youngnam(嶺南) region (the east area of the Korean peninsula).[4] In particular, this performance of Gopuri can be regarded as her own creative idea.

CHOI SUN STYLE

Choi Sun(崔仙) is a stage name. His real name is Choi Jung-Chul(崔正徹: 1935–). He was born in Jeon-Buk(全北) province, in the Honam region. He had learned the Korean traditional songs from his mother when he was very young. When he was about 10 years old, he entered a dance school, and finally began to learn the Gisang-Chum in a Gwonbeon in the city of Jeonju(全州). His teacher was a Gisang known as Kim Chu-Wol(金秋月).[5]

When he was twenty years old, he held his own performance in the city of Jeonju. And he opened a dance school with another dancer, Eun Bang-Cho. During that time, he danced wearing women's clothes because his movement is very feminine. This may have resulted from the fact that he learned dance from the Gisang in Gwonbeon.

His father was very stern, and did not want his son to be a dancer. However, Choi could not stop dancing. Choi recalls that his father finally said, "Go to your way," after seeing him perform a dance in women's clothing.[6] Korean society was not completely free from Confucian values until between the 1950s and 1960s, when Choi was in his twenties. In this situation, it was very difficult for a man to go to the ways of a dancer. Despite this, Choi never gave up his own way.

He participated in numerous dance performances with the famous dancers of that time. As a result, since the 1970s many people began to recognize him as a professional dancer. Choi received the second prize (though no first prize was awarded) in the 1st National Dance Contest in 1979, and the presidential prize in Gaechun(開天) Art Festival in 1984. And finally he was named a living human cultural treasure of Jeon-Buk Province (No. 15) in the field of Salpuri-Chum in 1996.

His Salpuri-Chum is called *Dongcho Salpuri-Chum* or *Honam Salpuri-Chum*. Choi explains the word Dongcho as originating from the two words, *Donggi*(童妓) and *Chorip*(草笠). Donggi means "young female dancer," and Chorip, "boy's traditional hat" or "boy who does not marry." Thus, he says that Dongcho means young male dancer.[7] This reflects that Dongcho Salpuri-Chum is a Salpuri-Chum performed by young boys.

Like Lee Mae-Bang, he wears a man's traditional white clothes; however, the long gown he wears is a little different from that worn by Lee. We call Lee's long gown Kwaeja, and Choi's, *Durumagi*. In fact, Kwaeja is the cloth of young boys, while Durumagi is the cloth of adults. If Dongcho Salpuri is a dance of young boys, it would make sense that the dancer wears Kwaeja. Despite this, the reason Cho wears Durumagi may be derived from the fact that Lee Mae-Bang has already worn Kwaeja. As a result, Choi, unlike Lee, wears a Chorip. It is very interesting.

Unlike other dancers, Choi likes to use a relatively short piece of fabric. Because the length of the fabric is short, he easily moves it as he wants. He sometimes puts the fabric on his shoulder and moves around the stage. Choi Sun's daughter, Choi Ji-Won, portraying the fabric as a rock, explains that her father, with a rock on his shoulder, dances heavily but delightfully; furthermore, she says, the fabric on his shoulder looks like the wing of a white crane.[8]

Choi places a large *Hwamunsuk*(花紋席), a Korean traditional colored carpet made of a kind of sedge, on the stage, and dances on it. His movements then are performed only on the Hwamunsuk. This is the main reason why the movements of his legs are not active compared with those of Lee Mae-Bang. Instead, the movements of his arms are very active. Especially, he likes to lift his arms up high and to use his shoulders. This can be also regarded as his own peculiarity. The movement of the shoulder is enough to promote the audience's Heung.

Because another name of his Salpuri-Chum is Honam Salpuri-Chum, the musical accompaniment of his Salpuri-Chum is based on the Honam Sinawi rhythm. However, the rhythm is relatively light, because his dance symbolizes a boy's actions. Accordingly, the set of musical instruments for the accompaniment is very simple.

He does not use the full set of Samhyunyookgak; rather, he dances according to the rhythm of Jangku, Jing, and *Kwangwari* (a kind of small gong). He also sometimes chants with his own Gueum. In this sense, we can say he created his own Salpuri-Chum, reflecting an element of the people's emotions in the Honam region (see Photos 15 and 16).

KIM BOK-RYUN STYLE

Kim Bok-Ryun(金福蓮: 1948–) was born in Gangwon(江原) province, located on the northeast side of South Korea. She learned the Korean traditional songs from her grandfather, and she first learned the dance, when she was about 10 years old, from her elementary school teacher. However, she did not continue studying dance during her middle and high school years. After graduating from high school, she married a military man. They moved to many different places as her husband was transferred to new assignments. Kim said she was very sick during that time, but she could not learn its cause. Many doctors said that her disease was a kind of nervous disease.[9]

When she moved into the city of Soowon(水原) in Gyeonggi province, she decided to start dancing, and became a student of Chung Gyung-Pa (鄭瓊坡), a famous traditional dancer. It was only after practicing dance again that she become healthy. Her disease might have been a kind of Sin-Byung.

In the Chosun dynasty there was a *Hwasung Jaeincheong*(華城才人廳). Hwasung is the old name of Soowon. A famous traditional artist there, whose name was Lee Dong-An(李東安: 1906–1965), tried to introduce many different artistic genres that were performed in Hwasung Jaeincheong. Chung Gyung-Pa, as a student of Lee, tried to reproduce Salpuri-Chum performed by the artists in the Jaeincheong. She finally became the living human cultural treasure of Gyeonggi Province (No. 8) in the field of Sapuri-Chum in 1991.

Unfortunately, Chung died in 2000, and Kim Bok-Ryun succeeded to Chung's title in 2002. Kim received the grand prize of art of Gyeonggi province in 2000, and she established the Association for Preservation of Hwasung Jaeincheong (華城才人廳保存會) after her teacher died.[10] She is now devoting herself to maintaining the dances of Hwasung Jaeincheong. Thus, her Salpuri-Chum is also called *Hwasung Jaeingcheong Salpuri-Chum.*

Kim wears women's traditional white clothing; however, the style of her clothes is a typical plebeian style. Like Kim Sook-Ja, she ties the waist with a piece of white fabric. The style of her clothes symbolizes the two kinds of people, ordinary people and shamans. In short, she harmonizes between the characters of ordinary people and that of shamans.

On this point, her Salpuri-Chum is a little different from that of Kim Sook-Ja, which focuses only on the shaman's movements. Moreover, unlike Kim Sook-Ja, Kim Bok-Ryun uses two pieces of white silk fabric. As mentioned earlier, Kim Sook-Ja uses a very long piece of fabric; however, Kim Bok-Ryun cuts the fabric into two pieces about 1.5 meters each in length. She uses the accompaniment of Samhyunyookgak, and the rhythm style is based on that of Kim Sook-Ja. She says: "Salpuri-Chum is a dance to solace the soul of the dead person who did not solve his/her Hahn; therefore, it represents grand and lofty world of spirit."[11] She tries to sublimate the wishes of the ordinary people as a lofty ideal.

Her steps are not splendid. Instead, she performs many movements with the two pieces of fabric. In the first part, she places a piece of fabric on the floor and holds another piece with her hand. She then performs an action symbolic of the two pieces being connected to each other. Sometimes, with the two pieces she makes the pattern *Taeguk*(太極), which is depicted in the national flag of Korea. The pattern means "Yin and Yang" or "sky and earth." The two pieces of fabric sometimes portrays the pattern of a whirlwind. She entwines and disentangles her body with the fabric; and similarly, she performs a shoulder dance by surrounding her shoulder with the fabric.

Kim Bok-Ryun likes to move forward and right-forward; however, she hesitates to move left-forward. This may result from her intent to represent the light aspect of our life and freedom.[12] In the Korean tradition, left as Yin means the dark aspect of all things. In this context, we can say that her Salpuri-Chum tries to demonstrate the light aspect of the Korean people's Hahn (see Photos 17 and 18).

KIM RAN STYLE

Kim, Ran(金蘭: 1943–) was born in the city of Gwangju(光州) in the Honam region. Her real name is Kim Geum-Hwa, and Kim Ran is her stage name. She had an aptitude for dance when she was very young. After graduating from high school in Gwangju, she went to Daejeon and became a student of Kim Sook-Ja. At that time, Kim Sook-Ja managed her own dance school in Daejeon. After Kim Sook-Ja left Daejeon, Kim Ran learned the traditional Korea dances in Seoul. She finally returned to Daejeon and opened her own dance school.

She presented her solo dance performance in 1965. She also composed the choreography for various national events, such as the final ceremony of the National Sports Competition in 1979, and the Korea National Dance Festival in 1980. In addition, she was president of the Daejeon Branch of the Korean Dance Association, and she established the Daejeon City Dane Company in 1985.[13] She finally became a living human cultural treasure of Daejeon Metropolitan City (No. 20) in the field of Salpuri-Chum in 2012.

Though a student of Kim Sook-Ja, Kim Ran's dance is different from that of her teacher. Like her teacher, she wears women's traditional white clothes; however, her clothes are more gorgeous than those of her teacher. And unlike her teacher and Kim Bok-Ryun, she does not tie a piece of white fabric around the waist. Also, she uses relatively short pieces of fabric, about 2.1 to 2.2 meters long and about 37 to 40 centimeters wide, compared to that used by her teacher. Moreover, her teacher dances by holding a long piece of fabric with both hands, while Kim Ran prefers to dance with the fabric only in one hand. In fact, her teacher danced in that manner—holding the fabric with only one hand—prior to being named the living human cultural treasure in 1990. Thus we can say that Kim Ran developed her teacher's old style.

Kim grasps the end of the fabric with the right hand and strokes the fabric with the left hand. We hardly see this kind of movement in other dances. Sometimes she also flies the fabric toward her face, and wraps her hand with the fabric. In another movement, she raises one of her arms to the height of her shoulder, and walks, putting the fabric over the raised arm. In this case, she performs the shoulder dance and moves backward with very light steps. Through this movement, she wants to represent the Korean people's Heung.

Because her dance originated with her teacher, the musical accompaniment of her dance is based on the Dosalpuri rhythm. Therefore, she moves very actively and nimbly around the stage. In other words, there are few static movements. However, the dance is felt differently from her teacher's dance because she likes to perform the repeated movements.

Most Salpuri-Chum dancers hesitate to perform repeated movements; however, Kim Ran wants to symbolize a certain image or spirit through the repetitions. In addition, her steps are more modernistic compared with her teacher's. And her nimble and sophisticated movements are very showy and flashy. Thus, her dance generally gives us some joyful and delighted feelings, although sometimes she tries to represent some sorrowful feelings (see Photos 19 and 20).

LEE EUN-JOO STYLE

Lee Eun-Joo (李銀珠: 1955–) was born in the city of Seoul. She started learning dance in elementary school. She had a special talent for the field of dance. During middle school, she received first prize in the National Student Dance Competition. She entered the Department of Dance of Soodo Women Teachers College (now Sejong University) in Seoul, where she met the famous Korean traditional dancer, Han Young-Sook. Han was a professor in the department at that time. In the university, she learned western ballet as well as the Korean traditional dances. As a university student, she also received the first prize in the National Dance Competition. After graduating from the university, she entered the graduate school in order to study dance more systematically. In graduate school, she worked as an assistant teacher under Professor Han.

After obtaining her master's degree, Lee taught dance in the Korea Traditional Music High School. She became a professor of Incheon Junior College in 1981 when she was only 26 years old, and was very successful in building her career until that time. However, her ambition to study dance did not stop. In particular, she wanted to study the theory of dance; but it was very difficult in Korea, until the 1970s, to find some meaningful books explaining systematically or theoretically Korean traditional dance. For that reason, she wanted to go to Europe and to study the theory of dance. In 1984, Lee decided to resign as professor at her college, and went to Germany, where she studied philosophy at Johann Wolfgang Goethe University-Frankfurt. Returning to Seoul in 1987, she again became a professor of Incheon Junior College in 1988.

Lee's study in Germany was very helpful in analyzing systematically the various movements of the Korean traditional dances. In 1994, she received the presidential prize in the 3rd National Dance Competition. And in 1998, she obtained her doctorate in dance from the Department of Physical Education of Sejong University. She became dean of the School of Art and Physical Education of the Incheon National University in 2014, and is currently a professor in the Department of Performing Arts of the University.

As mentioned earlier, Salpuri-Chum was recognized as a national intangible cultural treasure in 1990. However, Han Young-Sook died in 1989; therefore, she could not be a living human treasure although she greatly contributed to the development of Salpuri-Chum. Her grandfather, Han Sung-Jun, had virtually created the modern Salpuri-Chum. And Han, as his granddaughter, had led the main stream of Salpuri-Chum. Therefore, Lee Eun-Joo tried to introduce Han Young-Sook's Salpuri-Chum to the students.

Lee published the dance notation of Han Young-Sook style in 1992, the first presentation of dance movement in book form.[14] To show the style, she uses scenography. Also, in 1997, she established the Association for Preservation of Salpuri-Chum; in 2008, she changed its name to the Association for Preservation of Han Young-Sook Salpuri-Chum. In 2007, she published *The Thirty Three Dancers*, where she explained the lives and styles of the famous Korean traditional dancers who contributed to the development of Korean dance. And finally she became a living human cultural treasure of Seoul Special City (No. 46) in the field of Salpuri-Chum in 2015.

Like Han Young-Sook, Lee wears a woman's traditional white clothes, and uses a piece of white silk fabric, which measures 1.7 to 1.8 meters long, and forty-five centimeters wide. She argues that for keeping the natural waves of the fabric, its length has to be 10 centimeters longer than the dancer's height. She also uses the full set of Samhyunyookgak as the musical accompaniment of her dance; and the rhythm style of the accompaniment is nearly the same as that of her teacher, Han Young-Sook.

Strictly speaking, however, her style is different from that of her teacher. The most important difference lies in the fact that Lee uses all the joints of her body, such as those in the fingers, wrists, elbows, ankles, and knees. She applies the ways of using the body in ballet to the movements of Korean traditional dance. Therefore, her movements are more accurate than those of other dancers. For example, arms, hands, and legs keep an accurate angle in every movement.

The movements of the Korean traditional dances are relatively less accurate compared to those of ballet. In particular, the movements of Salpuri-Chum based on the Sinawi rhythm are likely to be improvisatorial in the process of representing Heung and sorrow. In this sense, we can say that Lee creates her own ways to use the body in the field of Salpuri-Chum. The accurate movements are likely to provoke a feeling of sternness. However, her movements are very natural.

Her movements are not excited and showy, because they are not based on exaggerated emotions. Also, she hesitates to walk nimbly and move widely. Further, she never flutters the fabric intentionally; she does not try to make a certain pattern with the fabric. Thus, the waves of the fabric are also very natural. The waves give us a free feeling. In sum, through her accurate but moderate movements, we can have some feelings simultaneously, such as sublimation, restraint of sorrow, and catharsis (see Photos 21, 22, 23, 24, 25, and 26).

NOTES

1. Eun-Joo Lee, *Thirty Three Dancers*, 165.
2. Ji-Won Kim, "The Local Characteristic of Kwon Myung-Hwa Salpuri-Chum in Daegu," in Byung-Ok Lee, *Salpuri-Chum: Styles and Lineage*, 425.
3. Eun-Joo Lee, *Thirty Three Dancers*, 162–63.
4. Ji-Won Kim, "Kwon Myung-Hwa Salpuri-Chum," 437.
5. Ji-Won Choi, "The Artistic Characteristic of Honam Salpuri-Chum," in Byung-Ok Lee, *Salpuri-Chum: Styles and Lineage*, 318.
6. Ibid., 314.
7. Eun-Joo Lee, *Thirty Three Dancers*, 174.
8. Ji-Won Choi, "Honam Salpuri-Chum," 317.
9. Eun-Joo Lee, *Thirty Three Dancers*, 293.
10. Hyun-Sook Shin, "A Study of Hwasung Jaeinchung Salpuri-Chum," in Byung-Ok Lee, *Salpuri-Chum: Styles and Lineage*, 356.
11. Eun-Joo Lee, *Thirty Three Dancers*, 297.
12. Hyun-Sook Shin, "Hwasung Jaeincheong Salpuri-Chum," 369.
13. Yeon-Hee Jang, "A Study of Kim Ran Salpuri-Chum as an Intangible Cultural Treasure of Daejeon Metropolitan City" (master's thesis, Mokwon University, 2013), 32.
14. Eun-Joo Lee, *Han Young Sook's Salpuri-Chum* (Seoul: Eunhachulpansa, 1992).

Chapter Seven

Salpuri-Chum and Other Korean Traditional Dances

OTHER KOREAN TRADITIONAL DANCES AS NATIONAL CULTURAL TREASURES

There are now a total of seven Korean traditional dances as national intangible cultural treasures. They are *Jinju Geom-Mu*(晋州劍舞), *Seungjeon-Mu* (勝戰舞), *Seung-Mu* (僧舞), *Cheoyong-Mu*(處容舞), *Hark-Yeonhwadae Hapsul-Mu*(鶴蓮花臺合設舞), *Taepyung-Mu*(太平舞), and *Salpuri-Chum*. We will briefly discuss here the six dances other than Salpuri-Chum, in order to understand more clearly the peculiarity of Salpuri-Chum, which is different from the other dances.

The first, Jinju Geom-Mu, a group dance by eight female dancers, was recognized as a national intangible cultural treasure (No. 12) in 1967. It is also called *Geomgi-Mu* or *Karl-Chum*. *Geom* means "sword," and *Gi*, "Gisang." The word *Karl*, as a pure Korean word, means "sword."

There are mainly two explanations for the origin of this dance. One states that it originated from the dance for mourning the young boys sacrificed for the nation in the kingdom of Silla. The other argues that it originated from the sword dance solacing the soul of Nongae(論介), a very famous Gisang in the Chosun dynasty. She threw herself into a river while holding onto a Japanese general during the *Yimjinwaeran*(壬辰倭亂), the war resulting from Japan's invasion of the Chosun dynasty in 1592–1598.

This dance has been performed since Yimjinwaeran. Its movements were detailed in the book, *Gakjeongjaemudoholgi*(各呈才舞圖笏記),[1] which documents with pictures the various performances by Gisang. Dancers wear the very colorful traditional battle dress, and dance with a white brass sword.

The musical instruments for the accompaniment of this dance are Piri, Jer (a kind of woodwind instrument), Haegeum, Jangku, and Buk.

The present Jinju Geom-Mu is based on the sword dance by Gisang belonging to the Gyobangcheong.[2] The eight dancers face each other standing in two lines, and perform the various movements holding a sword with each hand. The sword is a little different from the regular sword. The dancer can revolve it by its handle through the air; therefore, the sword can form the various shapes.

The movements are also varied. For example, the dancers turn around while bending their knees and sometimes sitting down on the ground or floor. This dance is recognized as a very meaningful cultural heritage, because the ways of using the sword and the movements of the dancer still keep the original form.

According to the Cultural Heritage Administration of Korea,[3] there were fifteen living human cultural treasures in this field; however, twelve of them died. Thus, there remain only two living human cultural treasures (Yoo Young-Hee: 劉永姬, and Kim So-Yeon: 金泰連), and an honorary living human cultural treasure (Chung Geun-Soon: 鄭今順). Also, there are a few assistants for instructing this dance.

The second, Seungjeon-Mu, is a group dance with a drum. This originated from a drum dance in the city of Tongyoung(統營), located in the southern area of the Korean peninsula. There was a naval base in Tongyoung during the Yimjinwaeran. At that time, Yi Sun-Sin(李舜臣: 1545–1598), a famous fleet commander who defeated a number of Japanese battleships, let his solders perform this dance to encourage them for victory in the war.[4] Because this dance was performed in the military base, it was named as the Seungjeon-Mu, a dance for celebrating the victory of war.

This dance could not be performed during the Japanese colonial period, because it was for celebrating victory over Japan. However, the formers Gisangs of Gyobangcheong such as Lee Gook-Hwa(李菊花), Kim Hae-Keun(金海根), and Chung Soon-Nam(鄭順男), researched the original forms and introduced this dance to the people.[5] This dance was finally recognized as a national intangible cultural treasure (No. 21) in 1968.

In performing this dance, the four main dancers wear red long traditional skirts, white traditional jackets, and Kwaeja. The jacket is very special. For example, a special sleeve is added to the end of the main sleeve of Jacket to cover the hands. We call it *Hansam*(汗衫). Also, the dancers wear different colored Kwaeja, according to the dancer's position: the dancer in the east wears a blue Kwaeja; the dancer in the west, a white one; the dancer in the south, a red one; and the dancer in the north, a black one.[6] In addition, each dancer wears a *Jokduri*, a kind of bride's headpiece.

With a drumstick in each hand, they perform the dance beating the big drum located in the center of the four directions (east, west, south, and north). The four dancers gather around the drum three times, and scatter to the four directions three times. Besides the four main dancers, twelve singers sing a song while turning around the main dancers. This dance is very similar to the court drum dance; thus, the structure of this dance is very solid.

The living human cultural treasures in this field did total ten persons; however, there are now only two persons (Han Chung-Ja: 韓貞子, and Erm Ok-Ja: 嚴玉子) holding the title, because the rest of them died.[7] Of course, there are several assistants for instructing this dance.

The third, Seung-Mu, is a type of Buddhist dance. Its origin is not clear. Simply, it is said that this dance is a secularized Buddhist dance developed for propagating Buddhism during the Chosun dynasty.[8] During that time, Buddhism was implicitly propagated because the dynasty accepted Confucianism as the ruling ideology. Thus, the Seung-Mu, without a determined structure, had been vaguely performed until Han Sung-Jun rearranged the dance.

After establishing the Institute of Chosun Music and Dance, Han Sung-Jun rearranged the Buddhist dance by mixing the rhythm of Buddhist ritual music with that of the shamanic ritual.[9] Han Young-Sook, Han's granddaughter, says; "*Bupgomu*(法鼓舞): a Buddhist ritual dance with a drum) was performed until 1912 when the Japanese government began to control the Chosun Buddhism through the law. Seung-Mu might be created on the basis of Bupgomu."[10] Han Sung-Jun tried to propagate this dance through his various performances. The dance was then taken up by Han Young-Sook, and it was recognized as a national intangible cultural treasure (No. 27) in 1987.

The dancer wears a traditional long blue skirt, and a wide long-sleeved white Buddhist robe. A male dancer wears the traditional men's white clothes. The dancer also wears a white peaked hat worn by Buddhist monks, and a wide red stole on the shoulders. The dancer, by fluttering the wide long-sleeved robe, performs the various movements. In particular, both of the long sleeves make very big, wide waves because the dancer holds a drumstick in each hand inside the sleeve.

However, when the dancer beats the drum, he or she takes the drumstick out of the sleeve. The speed and intensity of beating the drum standing on the floor varies greatly. Thus, most audiences join in with a storm of hand-clapping when the dancer beats the drum very fast. This scene produces the climax of the performance. The musical instruments used for the accompaniment are Piri, Daegeum, Haegeum, and Jangku, including a medium sized drum.

This dance is basically performed by one dancer. In this performance, the dancer shows two contradictory movements, active and passive. However, the two kinds of movements are finally harmonized. This reflects that the dance is focused on the sublimation of our fundamental sufferings. This dance partly reflects Buddhist thought through the rhythm connected to that of shamanic ritual. We can say that this dance sublimates the emotions of ordinary people into a Buddhist spirit.

The living human cultural treasures did total four persons; however, there is now only one person remaining (Lee Ae-Ju: 李愛珠) who keeps the title. There are also several assistants for instructing this dance.

The fourth, *Cheoyong-Mu*, has a very long history. This dance is based on a tale. Toward the end of the ninth century in the kingdom of Silla, a man whose name was Cheoyong found that an evil spirit spreading contagious disease tried to rape his wife. In this moment, he danced and sang a song. Upon hearing this song, the evil spirit disappeared.[11] After that, Cheoyong-Mu was performed in the court and local government on New Year's Eve to protect the people from the disease. In the kingdom of Koryeo, only one dancer performed this dance; however, from the era of the king Sejong in the Chosun dynasty, five dancers began performing it.[12] Therefore, it was a kind of court dance. Unfortunately, the dance was stopped during the Japanese colonial period.

In this dance, a mask symbolizing the face of Cheoyong is necessary. The mask looks very strange because it symbolizes a god to expel evil spirits. The five dancers wear the traditional colored clothes symbolizing east, west, south, north, and center. In Korean traditional society, every direction had its own color, as follows: blue meant east; white, west; red, south; black, north; and yellow, the center. The meaning of five directions is based on the theory of Ohaeng in Confucianism. This dance began as a court dance; it later came to be the people's entertainment. It was recognized as a national intangible cultural treasure (No. 39) in 1971. And finally, in 2009, it was inscribed on the representative list of the intangible cultural heritages in UNESCO.[13]

The movements of this dance are very gorgeous, active, and magnanimous. In short, the movements symbolize a powerful energy to expel evil spirits. In addition, this dance has another meaning—to pray for individual fortune as well as the prosperity of village and country. Even in the moment where the evil spirit tried to rape his wife, Cheoyong defeated the evil spirit by dancing and singing without agitation. This reflects the virtue of the Korean people based on Confucianism.

According to the Cultural Heritage Administration, there were seven living human cultural treasures in this field; however, there are now only two title holders (Kim Yong: 金龍, and Kim Joong-Sup: 金重燮) and one honorary human cultural treasure (Kim Chun-Heung: 金千興).[14] There are also three assistants to instruct this dance.

The fifth dance, *Hark-Yeonhwadae-Hapsul-Mu*(鶴蓮花臺合設舞), is a court dance in which Hark-Mu and Yeonhwadae-Mu are united. *Hark-Mu* is a white crane dance; in it, the dancer wears a crane-shaped mask. This dance was performed for the king in the kingdom of Koryeo. In the Chosun dynasty, a pair of dancers performed the dance wearing blue-and-yellow or white crane-shaped masks.[15]

This dance was not performed after the beginning of the 1900s; however, it was rearranged by Han Sung-Jun during the Japanese colonial period. Han relates that: "Wang San-Ak(王山岳) in the kingdom of Koguyreo created Germungo...Whenever he played the Germungo, a white crane came and danced. I created Hark-Chum on the basis of this story."[16] Han first performed this dance in Bumingwan in 1935.[17] This dance was taken up by Han Young-Sook, and in 1971 it was recognized as a national intangible cultural treasure (No. 40).

Yeonhwadae-Mu is based on a tale where two girls are reincarnated as two lotus flowers, and dance to repay their debts to the king.[18] In this dance, the two female dancers, wearing hats with a small bell, first hide themselves inside the lotus flower. When the flower is opened, they come out and dance in accordance with the musical accompaniment. This dance was integrated with Hark-Mu in 1995 and renamed Hark-Yeonhwadae-Hapsul-Mu.

This dance is performed by a total of ten dancers: one blue crane, one yellow crane, two main dancers, two assistant dancers, two persons with long bamboo poles, and two musicians. First, the two dancers wearing the crane masks dance their various movements. When the cranes pick the lotus flower, the two girls come out; and at this moment, the cranes fly away. The two persons with long bamboo poles sing a song, spreading toward the east and west directions. At this point, the two main dancers and two assistants begin dancing.

In this dance, the two dancers with crane-shaped masks perform the various movements almost the same as a crane. It is very difficult for a man or woman to portray realistically the various movements of a crane. Thus, its peculiarity is very meaningfully recognized. In addition, we can find that human beings and animals sympathize with each other in this dance. This suggests many different meanings to us.

The first living human cultural treasure in this field was Han Young-Sook. After she died, Lee Heung-Ku(李興九) succeeded to her title. At that time, the name was changed from Hark-Mu into Hark-Yeonhwadae-Hapsul-Mu. In addition to a title holder, there are now two assistants for instructing this dance.[19]

The sixth is *Taepyung-Mu*, a dance for supplication for peace and prosperity of the country. It was also created by Han Sung-Jun. For this dance, Han rearranged the shamanic dance of the Gyeonggi region. However, the dancer wears the clothes of a king or queen. In the case of a female dancer, her hairstyle is almost same as that of a queen. It is ironic.

Han says: "Although it is said that the dance of king is dance for king, I think that this dance performed by the king...I believe that this is Taepyung-Mu; thus, I teach this dance to my students."[20] This reflects that a shaman can be also a king because the ancient people identified a shaman with a king. Han as a lower-class person may suppose that ordinary people can be a king.

The musical accompaniment for this dance is based on the shamanic rhythm; however, it is regarded as a court dance. Therefore, its rhythm is very complicated and hard to play. According to the rhythms, the movements of the dancer are variously changed. The dancer sometimes walks slowly by using the backside of his foot or by lifting his knee. In particular, there is a lot of movements by using the legs. The steps of the dancer are very nimble and gorgeous.

There are three styles of this dance. The first is Han Young-Sook style. In this style, the dancer performs wearing the simple court clothes, and the movements are relatively moderate. The second is Kang Sun-Young(姜善泳) style, which is more showy than Han Young-Sook style. In this second style, the dancer performs at first wearing Hansam, a pair of extra sleeves; however, in the middle of the performance, the dancer gives the sleeve to the assistant and performs wearing only the regular court clothes. The third, Lee Dong-An style, is relatively simple compared to the other styles. In this style, the dancer performs wearing a man's blue court clothes with the traditional hat of a governmental officer. The dancer also wears Hansam.

Taepyung-Mu was recognized as a national intangible cultural treasure (No. 92) in 1988. At this time, Kang Sun-Young became the first living cultural treasure. As a result, Han Young-Sook style and Lee Dong-An style were not recognized as national cultural treasures. However, those styles continue to be performed by their students. Unfortunately, Kang Sun-Young died in 2016, so there is now no living human cultural treasure. Of course, there are three assistants for instructing the Kang Sun-Young style.[21]

SALPURI-CHUM DISTINGUISHED FROM OTHER DANCES AND ITS CURRENT SITUATION

As explained above, the six dances listed as national cultural treasures were basically court dances. Although the rhythm of Seung-Mu and Taepyung-Mu is partly based on that of shamanic ritual, its main characteristics are absolutely different from Sinawi rhythm. Those dances have a prescribed sheet of music; therefore, there cannot be improvisatorial elements in the musical accompaniment. Of course, the speed of the rhythm of those dances is based on the rhythm of the Korean traditional music, which starts very slowly and gradually becomes faster. But the players of the musical instruments have to follow the sheet music. And the dancers then have no opportunities to display their improvisatorial movements.

In Salpuri-Chum, the dancer becomes a conductor, and the players of the musical instruments follow her steps and movements. But in other dances, the dancers have to follow the directions of the players of the musical instruments. This is the first difference between Salpuri-Chum and other dances. In this context, we can say that Salpuri-Chum originated from the shamanic dance, while the other dances are types of court dances performed on the basis of the sheet music.

Next, Salpuri-Chum is basically a solo dance. But Jinju Geom-Mu, Seungjeon-Mu, and Cheoyoung-Mu, are group dances. Seung-Mu and Taepyung Mu are a kind of solo dance; yet these two dances are also sometimes performed as a group dance. Of course, Salpuri-Chum can be performed as a group dance. But this is likely to impair its distinctive role in expelling evil spirits. This is a second difference between Salpuri-Chum and other dances.

A third difference is in the meaning of the dances. Jinju Geom-Mu and Seungjeon-Mu are dances basically to celebrate victory in war. Cheoyong-Mu is a kind of mask dance. Hark-Yeonhwadae-Hapsul-Mu is a kind of dance representing the sympathetic communication between human beings and other animals. Seung-Mu is a type of Buddhist dance, although Han Sung-Jun added to it some elements of Korean folk music. Taepyung-Mu can be also regarded as a court dance for the palace, to celebrate and supplicate peace and prosperity for the country. Therefore, the main meaning of Salpuri-Chum is absolutely different from that of other dances.

Fourth, Salpuri-Chum uses a piece of fabric. In this dance, the meaning of the fabric is an essential element. If the dancer does not use a piece of fabric, even though the dance's movements are based on those of Salpuri-Chum, we cannot say the dance is Salpuri-Chum. Other dances do not use this kind of fabric. In Seung-Mu and Taepyung-Mu, the dancer wears very-long-sleeved clothes and an extra sleeve; however, the main characteristic of the sleeves is different from that of the piece of fabric in Salpuri-Chum.

Fifth, the dancer of Salpuri-Chum wears white clothes. But the dancers in other kinds of dances wear very colorful and gorgeous clothes. A female dancer in Salpuri-Chum has a very simple hair style, which is same as the typical style of ordinary women. Of course, the male dancer of Salpuri-Chum wears a traditional hat, but its style is also based on that of ordinary people. This reflects that Salpuri-Chum is a dance for ordinary people, not for the noble class and royal family. Thus, we can say that Salpuri-Chum is a typical dance reflecting the emotions of ordinary people.

As mentioned earlier, three leading dancers created the three main styles of Salpuri-Chum: Han Young-Sook, Lee Mae-Bang, and Kim Sook-Ja. Unfortunately, all of them have died, and there is currently no title holder for national living human cultural treasure. Instead, there are five local living human cultural treasures in this field. Given this situation, we should discuss the styles of Salpuri-Chum.

As just noted, there were at first three styles. Because of circumstances, Han Young-Sook could not be a living human cultural treasure in this field, even though she succeeded to the style of her grandfather, who first arranged this dance. It is said that Sinawi rhythm can be broadly classified into Gyeonggi Sinawi rhythm and Honam Sinawi rhythm. If so, Han and Kim danced based on the former rhythm, and Lee on the latter rhythm. More specifically, Kim danced in accordance with the rhythm of Dodang-Gut, which is related to Gyeonggi Sinawi rhythm. However, her movements represent directly the shamanic movements, while Han's movements are very moderate, following the major rhythm of Gyeonggi Sinawi.

Despite these differences, there was no national living human cultural treasure in Han Young-Sook style because she died before Salpuri-Chum was recognized as an intangible national cultural treasure. However, the other two dancers, Lee and Kim, were able to be national living cultural treasures. If Han's style can be regarded as a meaningful style in this field, the government had to select a dancer succeeding her style. However, the government did not select a living national cultural treasure of her style, in spite of the fact that many students are continually learning the style in the various dance schools, including the universities.

In this situation, Seoul Special City finally recognized Han Young-Sook Style as an intangible cultural treasure of the city. And Lee Eun-Joo first became a living human cultural treasure of Seoul Special City in this field in 2015. This provided a good opportunity to reactivate Han Young-Sook style, even though it has not been recognized yet as an intangible national cultural treasure. Of course, since Lee Mae-Bang and Kim Sook-Ja died, their successors to those titles have not been selected. However, their situations are somewhat different from that of Han Young-Sook, because they first became living human national cultural treasures in the field of Salpuri-Chum.

Apart from these three styles, we also have to discuss the styles of Salpuri-Chum as local cultural treasures. The styles of Kwon Myung-Hwa and Choi Sun are different from the Lee Mae-Bang style, although all three are based on the Honam Sinawi music. Of course, the styles of Kwon and Choi also differ from each other. The styles of Kim Bok-Ryun and Kim Ran differ as well from the style of their teacher, Kim Sook-Ja, and also differ from each other. Further, the style of Lee Eun-Joo is different from that of her teacher, Han Young-Sook, even though she became a living human cultural treasure of Seoul Special City in the field of Han Young-Sook style.

These differences derived from the dancers' thoughts and their physical conditions. In order to discuss these differences, we have to first consider the meaning of imitation and its limit in art. Furthermore, we have to discuss the meaning of creation.

The great artistic works in history still move our emotions. Thus, we can have a wish to imitate the works. Psychoanalytically, this is based on the ego ideal which wants to experience again the pleasure which it once enjoyed. This is the primary narcissistic wish, the wish to return to the mother's womb.[22] Thus, the many great works are continually imitated. In this sense, the three main styles in Salpuri-Chum will continue to be presented as long as they move our emotions.

However, the three main styles cannot be imitated without differences. According to the dancers' spiritual and physical condition, the styles can be different from their teachers' styles even though they want to imitate exactly their teacher's styles. This is the limit of imitation. For example, the melodies of Beethoven and Mozart still move our emotions; therefore, many musicians want to play their melodies. However, each performer gives us different feelings even if they play the same melody.

In this context, the peculiarities of the various styles of the local cultural treasures in the field of Salpuri-Chum have to be recognized as their own styles. In fact, the various local styles have their own peculiarities beyond the imitation of their teacher's dance. This means that they create their own style. This is reason why the Salpuri-Chum of Han Young-Sook is called "Han Young-Sook style," despite the fact that she succeeded to her grandfather's style. This is the same in the case of the other dances.

In fact, it is not reasonable to classify styles according to their teachers for the reason that they first created their own style. If we classify all styles of Salpuri-Chum only into the three main styles, variety as an essential element of art cannot be realized. We have to consider that variety can be a basis for creation. In particular, variety cannot be avoided when we consider the improvisatorial elements of the Salpuri-Chum.

This does not mean that the three main styles are meaningless. Nobody can deny that the three styles have greatly contributed to the development of modern Salpuri-Chum. Therefore, we need to understand their peculiarities, and hand down their beauties to posterity. However, it is natural to bring forth various new styles in the process of imitating the main styles. It is an inevitable result. Through this process, the new styles can be created even though the basic forms are not changed. There are no purely or perfectly new forms in this world.

NOTES

1. *Encyclopedia of Korean Culture*, s.v. "정재무도홀기" (Jeongjaemudoholgi), accessed October 19, 2016, http://terms.naver.com/entry.nhn?docId=795499&cid=46666&categoryId=46666.

2. *The Electric Dictionary of Korean Local Culture*, s.v. "진주검무" (Jinju Geom-Mu), ed. The Academy of Korean Studies(한국학중앙연구원: www.aks.ac.kr), accessed October 19, 2016, http://terms.naver.com/entry.nhn?docId=2632614&cid=51942&categoryId=54845.

3. "Jinju Geom-Mu(진주검무)," *Cultural Heritage Administration* (http://www.cha.go.kr/), accessed October 19, 2016, http://www.cha.go.kr/ccomBasi/ccomBasiJunsList.do?ccjuKdcd=17&ccjuAsno=00120000&ccjuCtcd=38.

4. "Seungjeon-Mu(승전무)," *Cultural Heritage Administration*, accessed October 19, 2016, http://www.cha.go.kr/korea/heritage/search/Culresult_Db_View.jsp?mc=NS_04_03_01&VdkVgwKey=17,00210000,38.

5. *Encyclopedia of Korean Culture*, s.v. "승전무" (Seungjeon-Mu), accessed October 19, 2006, http://terms.naver.com/entry.nhn?docId=559573&cid=46666&categoryId=46666.

6. Ibid.

7. "Seungjeon-Mu(승전무)," *Cultural Heritage Administration*, accessed October 19, 2016, http://www.cha.go.kr/ccomBasi/ccomBasiJunsList.do?ccjuKdcd=17&ccjuAsno=00210000&ccjuCtcd=38.

8. *Encyclopedia of Korean Culture*, s.v. "승무" (Seung-Mu), accessed October 19, 2016, http://terms.naver.com/entry.nhn?docId=559527&cid=46666&categoryId=46666.

9. Hwa-Jin Oh, *A History of Korean Dance through the Study of Dancers* (Seoul: Yeoronsa, 1992), 43–44.

10. Ibid., 44.

11. *Junior's Encyclopedia*(어린이백과), s.v. "처용무" (Cheoyong-Mu), by Lee Hung-Jun, provided by Sigongjunior(시공주니어), accessed October 19, 2016, http://www.sigongsa.com/junior/juniorMain.php.

12. Ibid.

13. "Cheoyongmu," *UNESCO*, accessed October 19, 2016, http://www.unesco.org/culture/ich/en/RL/cheoyongmu-00189.

14. "Cheoyong-Mu(처용무)," *Cultural Heritage Administration*, accessed October 19, 2016, http://www.cha.go.kr/ccomBasi/ccomBasiJunsList.do?ccjuKdcd=17&ccjuAsno=00390000&ccjuCtcd=11.

15. *Encyclopedia of Korean Culture*, s.v. "학연화대합설무" (Hark-Yeonhwadae-Hapsul-Mu), accessed October 19, 2016, http://terms.naver.com/entry.nhn?docId=532171&cid=46666&categoryId=46666.

16. Hwa-Jin Oh, *History through the Study of Dancers*, 51.

17. See note 15 above.

18. "Hark-Yeonhwadae-Hapsul-Mu(학연화대합설무)," *Cultural Heritage Administration*, accessed October 19, 2016, http://search.cha.go.kr/srch_new/search/search_top.jsp?searchCnd=&searchWrd=&home=total&mn=&gubun=search&query=%ED%95%99%EC%97%B0%ED%99%94%EB%8C%80%ED%95%A9%EC%84%A4%EB%AC%B4&x=14&y=14.

19. "Hark-Yeonhwadae-Hapsul-Mu(학연화대합설무)," *Cultural Heritage Administration*, accessed October 19, 2016, http://www.cha.go.kr/ccomBasi/ccomBasiJunsList.do?ccjuKdcd=17&ccjuAsno=00400000&ccjuCtcd=11.

20. Hwa-Jin Oh, *History through the Study of Dancers*, 48.

21. "Taepyung-Mu(태평무)," *Cultural Heritage Administration*, accessed October 19, 2016, http://www.cha.go.kr/ccomBasi/ccomBasiJunsList.do?ccjuKdcd=17&ccjuAsno=00920000&ccjuCtcd=ZZ.

22. Yong-Shin Kim, *Psychoanalytic Interpretation of Art*, 80–86.

Chapter Eight

Aesthetics of Salpuri-Chum

PHILOSOPHY AND ARTISTIC FORM OF SALPURI-CHUM

So far we have been discussing various aspects of Salpuri-Chum. In this part, we will first summarize its philosophical meanings, and then we can illustrate the artistic form of Salpuri-Chum. In the first chapter, we have already considered the forms of art; therefore, the characterization of artistic form will be based on that discussion.

First, Salpuri-Chum reflects the Korean people's belief system about life and death. For the Korean people, there is no clear distinction between these two concepts. As mentioned earlier, death means to return to the original place from which we have come; moreover, the soul of the dead person has influence on living persons. This belief brings forth two principles.

The first principle is respect for ancestors. The Korean traditional people believed that the soul of the dead person could go to the highest sky if he or she accumulated good deeds in this world. Once the soul of dead person goes to the highest place, it has a strong power to influence living persons. In this case, the soul can be regarded as a god.

In addition to the good deeds, the soul of a dead person can attain the highest sky if it is buried in Myungdang. Therefore, most people try not only to accumulate good deeds in this world, but also to be buried in Myungdang. The living persons, then, pray to the soul which becomes a god to solve their problems. This kind of belief promotes the practice of ancestor worship. It reflects the mutual interests between the living and the dead.

Everyone wants to accumulate good deeds in this world in order to be a god after dying. Also, to be buried in Myungdang, everyone has to love their family members, because the final decision to bury the dead person in Myungdang depends upon his living family members. Furthermore, the living family members receive many benefits from their ancestor whose soul has gone to the highest sky. In this view, the relations between the dead person and the living person cannot be broken.

The second principle is to solve or solace regrets of the dead person though the Gut. If the soul of a dead person has regrets, it is likely to be an evil spirit, and it will harm living persons who are closely related to the dead person as it moves around the air. Therefore, the living people have to solve or pacify the regrets of dead person.

The Gut has two meanings. One is to solve the regrets of dead person. It is good for the dead person because he can go to the higher sky through the Gut. It is also good for the living because the evil spirit cannot harm them once its regrets are solved or pacified. Thus we can say the Salpuri-Gut is a ritual for the dead person as well as the living persons. But there is also another meaning: this is to pray to the soul of the person who has accumulated good deeds in this world and gone to the highest sky by his own efforts, to solve the living people's problems. This is also closely related to our wish, dream, and expectations, based on our ego ideal.

Second, Salpuri-Chum represents the essential elements of the Korean people's emotions. These are Hahn and Jeong. As explained earlier, the Hahn has two aspects; the bright and the dark. On the one hand, the Hahn is sublimated through Salpuri-Chum. On the other hand, it provides the Korean people with an opportunity to love even their Hahn. The Korean people try to sublimate their Hahn, while they also sometimes try to love their Hahn.

This kind of paradoxical feeling is closely connected to the concept of Jeong in which love and hate co-exist. A Korean person may hate someone because he or she loves him or her, while he or she may love someone because he or she hates him or her. It is very contradictory. In contrast to western psychoanalytic theory, the contradiction between love and hate does not exist in the Korean people's minds. In other words, these two feelings cannot be separated from each other; they exist as one feeling in their minds.

There is also a practice of waiting in the process of changing hate into love. Korean people try to wait for the lover, who has left them, to return. But if the lover does not return, they try to sustain their love by pacifying the distressed mind toward the one who left them. This process also means waiting until the mind is calmed. At first glance, it seems that the two feelings are separated from each other, if a waiting process is needed for the change of mind. However, these two feelings are not separated from each other, because the waiting process is not needed if there is no feeling of love from the start.

Without understanding this kind of complicated emotional dynamics, it is very difficult to illustrate the essential meaning of Salpuri-Chum. It represents not only love but also hate. The Korean people who have lots of Hahn hate their destiny; however, they simultaneously try to create a new destiny by loving their Hahn. The Korean people continually change their destiny by solving or sublimating their Hahn. Moreover, they also continually try to find happiness in their minds through the waiting process to love their destiny.

Psychoanalytically, the effort to solve the problems through the Salpuri ritual may be regarded as a projection which tries to impute one's problems to other people. It can also be said that waiting for the lover who has left is very passive. However, these interpretations cannot be applied to the Korean people's emotional dynamics. The Korean people continually try to find their own happiness in their minds through the Salpuri ritual. It is, then, an effort to create their happiness. Accordingly, this cannot be simply regarded as a regressive attitude. Through this ritual, their sorrow changes into the Heung, and the Heung provides the Korean people with the energy to cultivate and create their new destiny by overcoming their problems.

Third, Salpuri-Chum represents the free spirit of the ordinary people. It is not a dance for the royal and noble class. Among the seven dances of the intangible national cultural treasures, only Salpuri-Chum is the plebeian dance. It is a dance to represent the free spirit by solving the ordinary people's Hahn and by emitting the ordinary people's Heung.

This characteristic is clearly represented through the Sinawi rhythm. As mentioned earlier, only Salpuri-Chum is based on the Sinawi rhythm, which has no sheet music or an accurate metronome. The players play their instruments according to their feelings. However, their feelings depend upon the dancer's movement. This encourages the improvisatorial movements and rhythm. This element is not in court dances.

The improvisatorial element of Sinawi rhythm is based on the emotional dynamics of the Korean people. The Korean traditional people sang and danced when they met problems as well as when they felt happiness. Their songs and dances did not have a strict form. They pleaded their sad situation to the sky, and enjoyed their happiness in the reality. Their lamentation and joyfulness made the various songs and dances. In this case, sheet music and regular movement were needless. This way of representing their feelings was very improvisatorial. The Sinawi rhythm originated from this situation; and this rhythm was used for the shamanic ritual and produced the shamanic dances.

The improvisatorial element provides the dancers and the players of the musical instruments with the opportunities to manifest their free spirit. We pray to the gods for our happiness, in order to free us from our sufferings. To solace the regrets of evil spirits is also to free them from their regrets. Therefore, Salpuri-Chum can be regarded as a dance for realizing freedom in the minds of ordinary people. In short, the improvisatorial element can be a useful means to realize the free spirit.

In fact, Salpuri-Chum was derived from the improvisation of the Sinawi rhythm and the shamanic movements which reflected the emotional dynamics of the Korean people. Of course, Han Sung-Jun standardized the improvisatorial elements for the modern theatrical Salpuri-Chum. Even so, the spirit of the improvisation does not disappear. For example, the players of Sinawi rhythm still adjust the tone of the rhythm according to the dancer's movements. In this process, the dancer and the players make a wonderful harmony improvisatorially.

Furthermore, the audiences become the assistants of the dancers and the players in the performance of Salpuri-Chum. They feel sorrow and pleasure together with the dancer and the players. This means that Salpuri-Chum, unlike the western ballet, is not a performance just to watch the dancer's movements and to hear the players' rhythm. The audiences participate emotionally together with the dancer and the players in the performance of Salpuri-Chum. This is the reason we can say that Salpuri-Chum is a Korean-styled plebeian dance.

When we consider the three characteristics mentioned above, the artistic form of Salpuri-Chum becomes clear. It is not an art to seek perfection. The western ballet tries to present perfect motion. In the ballet, the dancers stand and walk using only the end of their toes on the floor. It is impossible for ordinary people. Their physical condition is also almost perfect. The audiences feel satisfaction through this perfection. Therefore, we can say that one of essential elements of the western ballet is derived from our wish to realize perfection. This is the reason why there cannot be any improvisatorial movement in the western ballet.

Salpuri-Chum, however, does not try to seek perfection. There is no clear difference between the dancer's clothes and ordinary people's clothes. Also, most ordinary people can imitate basically the dancer's movements. The dancer does not perform movements which the ordinary person cannot imitate. But the movements move our emotions because these are based on our lives in reality. If Salpuri-Chum does not seek perfection or truth, it is clear that this dance reflects our reality. In this case, there are two ways to reflect our reality: one is to sublimate our problems in the reality, and another is to love our reality. Salpuri-Chum reflects both of them.

Regarding the sublimation, we can solve our Hahn through the Salpuri ritual. For example, to call on a god to solve our problems can be compared with finding an hallucination in psychoanalytic theory. We can partly solve our problems in hallucination. All kinds of wishes based on the hallucination cannot be regarded as regressive or perverted behaviors. Some of them can be forms of sublimation, because some sorrows or problems derived from our original limits can be pacified and resolved through hallucination. We can pacify or resolve our sorrow and problems by calling on some gods. The positive function of religion may be an example of this case. If so, this is based on our beliefs; therefore, this can be instead regarded as sublimation. In short, Salpuri-Chum exhibits a kind of artistic form based on sublimation.

Regarding love of our problems, Salpuri-Chum reflects our narcissism in which we love our sorrows and problems. Psychoanalytically, we can pacify our problems by loving them. This is a way to solace ourselves. If we cannot solve our problems in reality, we can overcome the problems by loving them. This is based on Freud's constancy principle. For self-preservation, our minds have to be stable. For this condition, narcissism functions as a positive role. In the Salpuri ritual, we can call on the gods as well as enjoy our situation on the basis on our Heung. In fact, we can solve our sorrow through the Heung. This is based on narcissism.

Moreover, we can represent our sorrow through the Salpuri ritual. When we tell our problems to a god, we cry. When we hear the evil spirit's regrets through this ritual, we also cry together. And then we laugh, when we think that our problems are solved. Once we have cried and laughed, our emotions are partly purified. In other words, we can feel catharsis through this situation. Therefore, Salpuri-Chum gives us an opportunity to pacify our sorrow and promote our pleasure through the catharsis.

For the Korean people, catharsis is also related to their emotional dynamics. We cry because we hate our lover who left us. In this case, the tears are based on the feeling of hate. But, there can be another situation in which we cry because we cannot forget that our lover left us. In this case, the tears are based on the feeling of love. This means that the catharsis of the Korean people is also derived from the conflicting emotions.

This kind of aspect based on catharsis is also closely related to the narcissistic aspect. When we consider the Korean people's emotional dynamics in which love and hate coexist, this relation is more clearly explained. For instance, they can hate their problems; however, they can also love them. This is based on the paradoxical emotions of the Korean people. In this context, Salpuri-Chum also takes an artistic form of narcissism and catharsis.

THE BEAUTY OF SALPURI-CHUM

Beyond the philosophical meanings and the artistic forms of Salpuri-Chum, we can find various beautiful scenes in the dance. The scenes are enough to move our emotions. We can summarize the artistic beauties as follows:

First, one of the artistic beauties in Salpuri-Chum is derived from the clothes of the dancer. Korean traditional clothes are very wide and long. In the case of a female dancer, she wears the very wide and long skirt. She also wears a jacket with wide sleeves. A male dancer wears the traditional pants, unlike a female dancer; but the pants are very wide. In addition, he wears a jacket with wide sleeves and a long gown.

In western ballet, the audiences can directly see the dancer's body line and its movements. As mentioned earlier, the perfect body condition of a dancer is enough to move our emotions desiring to find perfection or truth. However, the audiences of Salpuri-Chum cannot directly see the dancer's body line and its movements. In other words, the movements of the dancer's foot, knee, leg, and arm, are not directly seen in Salpuri-Chum. Thus, the audiences can see only the movements presented through the outside of the clothes.

In fact, the actual movements of the dancer's body are hidden in Salpuri-Chum. However, the dancer creates some smooth and refined movements through the clothes. It can be called "the indirect effect of beauty." The audiences cannot see the perfection of the dancer's physical condition in this dance. Instead, they can enjoy another artistic beauty through the moderate movements. The dancer's actual body movements are purified through the clothes.

Our emotions can be moved not only by direct explanation, but also by indirect explanation. In this sense, we can say that the western ballet seeks the direct explanation, while Salpuri-Chum seeks the indirect explanation. This is also compared with the meaning of line. Most people like straight lines; however, they also like wavy lines. If the western ballet is compared with the straight line, Salpuri-Chum is the wavy line.

There is another aspect related to the clothes: this is the direction of the movements. In the western ballet, the dancer likes to perform upward movements. Therefore, the movements are very active. But most dancers in Salpuri-Chum hesitate to perform upward movements because of the clothes. Rather, they like to perform downward movements. This is why their movements seem to be passive.

Second, the harmony between two contradictory elements is one of the artistic beauties which the Salpuri-Chum seeks. As we have explained, Salpuri-Chum represents simultaneously sorrow and pleasure. These two contradictory emotional feelings are ingeniously harmonized in Salpuri-Chum. This is possible because of the Korean people's Jeong as a contradictory feeling. In this harmony, love and hate are not separated from each other. This is the reason why Salpuri-Chum takes simultaneously the two forms of art, sublimation and narcissism or catharsis.

We can also find this harmony in the movements of Salpuri-Chum. When we discuss the artistic beauty derived from the clothes, we say that the movements seem to be passive. But, this is the aspect reflected through the clothes. The body movements of the dancer are very active inside the clothes. Thus, it can be understood as the harmony between activity and passivity by means of the clothes.

The Korean people have an expression: *Jung-Joong-Dong*(靜中動). *Jung* means "standstill," and *Dong*, "movement. In addition, *Joong* means "center" or "in." Thus, these words mean "the movement in the standstill," or "the standstill in the movement." The dancers of Salpuri-Chum try to represent the meaning of Jung-Joong-Dong in their performance. Even though they do not move, they want to show some movement. It is very difficult to represent this harmony. In short, the dancers need very high skill.

To acquire this skill, the dancers first learn the ways of keeping the body in balance. For instance, the dancers have to stand without moving, though the posture of their bodies inside the clothing is tilted toward a certain direction. The tilted posture is the first action to move; thus, the tilted motion in the standstill position while balancing can be a way to present the Jung-Joong-Dong. Their moderate movements can be also understood as a harmony between the standstill and the active movements.

This harmony can be found in the relation between the rhythm of the accompaniment and the dancer's movements. As we have pointed out in the three main styles of Salpuri-Chum, the dancer makes moderate movements under the major rhythm. We can see this harmony in the Han Young-Sook style. However, the dancer's movements are relatively nimble and showy under the minor rhythm. This is the Lee Mae-Bang style. We can also find this kind of harmony in other styles.

If the artists focus only on the harmony between two contradictory elements, they are likely to lose a certain distinctiveness. Therefore, harmony is a very difficult subject in art. This means that the artists need their own particular philosophy and skill, if people are to perceive the artistic beauty in the harmony the dancers seek. In this sense, the Salpuri-Chum provides us with an opportunity to enjoy the ingenious as well as skillful harmony between two contradictory elements.

Third, one of the artistic beauties of Salpuri-Chum is produced by the piece of long white fabric. It is hard to find any other dance performed with a piece of fabric. The fabric symbolizes soul, spirit, wish, dream, expectation, and so forth. We have already discussed the symbolic meaning of the fabric in terms of philosophy and psychoanalysis. Apart from the symbolic meaning, the fabric contributes to the creation of the various beautiful patterns.

Dancers use the special fabric for creative patterns in different ways. For example, the length and width of the piece of fabric can be different, according to the dancer. Also, some dancers use a single piece of fabric, while others use two. This reflects that the fabric is a very important tool to represent some beautiful scenes beyond its symbolic meaning.

Some dancers try to create some patterns with the fabric intentionally. In this case, the symbolic meaning of the fabric is clearer. These symbolic patterns are enough to move our emotions. However, others just flutter and wave the fabric without any intended pattern. In this case, the patterns which the fabric creates are very natural. These natural patterns are also enough to move our emotions. In this view, the fabric is a necessary tool for the Salpuri-Chum.

As mentioned earlier, if the dancer does not use the fabric, it cannot be regarded as a Salpuri-Chum. This means that the movements without fabric lose not only the symbolic meaning of Salpuri-Chum, but also the artistic beauty created through the various patterns. If so, the fabric can then be regarded as a tool to harmonize between the symbolic meaning and the artistic beauty in Salpuri-Chum.

Fourth, the improvisatorial element of Salpuri-Chum can also create an artistic beauty. As mentioned earlier, this element is derived from the Sinawi rhythm. It has no sheet music; moreover, it does not keep a regular marked beat. In this rhythm, the dancer becomes the conductor. Therefore, the dancer and the players make the beautiful harmony improvisatorially. This kind of harmony cannot be manifested in other Korean traditional dances. Improvisation is one of the main characteristics of the Korean people's emotional dynamics. In this sense, Salpuri-Chum can be regarded as the most representative dance to reflect precisely the essential characteristic of the Korean people's unconscious.

However, the improvisation may sometimes hurt a certain order of the performance. Also, it is likely to be connected to some secular movements which may damage the pure artistic beauty. Therefore, the dancers and players have to be careful in the demonstration of their improvisatorial movements.

Fifth, the artistic beauty is also variously created through the differing styles of Salpuri-Chum. Each style creates its own beauty, despite the fact that the basic structure of the dance is not changed. In particular, the dancer's reflection of the rhythm of accompaniment, as well as the shape and length of the piece of fabric, contribute to the creation of many styles which can be regarded as distinct. As we have pointed out in discussing the main styles and other styles of Salpuri-Chum, the harmony between the dancer's movements and the musical accompaniment is created in various ways. The patterns made when the dancer uses a single piece of fabric are also absolutely different from those made with two pieces of fabric. The patterns created also vary, according to the length of the fabric.

The dancer's various actions in pursuing a particular style, however, may hurt the main characteristic of Salpuri-Chum. Thus, dancers have to try to keep the essential characteristics of Salpuri-Chum. If the movements are created without keeping the basic structure of Salpuri-Chum, or without considering the essential characteristics of the dance, the dance cannot be recognized as a meaningful style of Salpuri-Chum.

Despite this problem, the styles function as positive roles in the development and propagation of Salpuri-Chum, insofar as the dancers do not lose the essential meaning of Salpuri-Chum. The art's life force lies in its creation, and the artistic creations are derived from the varieties. In this sense, the styles of Salpuri-Chum will provide us with many meaningful artistic beauties. Furthermore, they will introduce us to the various imaginary worlds in which we can be free from our sufferings, through sublimation, narcissism, and catharsis.

Bibliography

KOREAN PUBLICATIONS

Alford, Fred. *Korean Values in the Age of Globalization*(한국인의 심리에 관한보고서). Translated by Kyung-Tae Nam. Seoul: Greenbee(그린비), 2000.
Association of Korean Folklore(한국민속학회). *The Understanding of the Korean Folklore*(한국민속학의 이해). Seoul: Munhak Academy(문학 아카데미), 1994.
Bokyung-Munhwasa(보경문화사), ed. *Sunglidaejeon*(性理大全). Seoul: Bokyung-Munhwasa, 1994.
Cho, Heung-Yoon(조흥윤). *The Korean Shamans*(한국의 무). Seoul: Jungeumsa(정음사), 1983.
Cho, Heung-Yoon(조흥윤), Lee Bo-Hyung(이보형), and Kim Soo-Nam(김수남). *Seoul Jinogwi-Gut*(서울 진오귀굿). Seoul: Yeolhwadang(열화당), 1993.
Choi, Gil-Sung(최길성). *Study of the Korean Shamanism*(한국무속의 연구). Seoul: Asia Munwhasa(아시아문화사), 1978.
Choi, Tae-Hyun(최태현). "Musical Condition of Sinawi and Its Background(시나위 명칭배경과 음악적 조건)." *Journal of the Society for Korean Historico-Musicology* (한국음악사학보) (Seoul: The Society for Korean Historico-Musicology) 35 (December 2005): 117–136.
Chun, Yi-Du(천이두). *A Study on the Structure of Hahn*(한의 구조연구), Seoul: Munhak & Jisung(문학과 지성사), 1993.
Chung, Bum-Tae(정범태). *Dance and the Dancers*(춤과 그 사람). Seoul: Yeolhwadang(열화당), 1992.
Chung, Bum-Tae(정범태) and Koo Hee-Seo(구희서). *The Famous Dancers in Korea*(한국의 명무). Seoul: Hankook Ilbo Press (한국일보출판국), 1985.
———. *Han Young-Sook's Salpuri*(한영숙 살풀이). Seoul: Yeolhwadang(열화당), 1992.
———. *Kim Sook-Ja's Dosalpuri*(김숙자 도살풀이). Seoul: Yeolhwadang(열화당), 1992.
Chung, Byung-Ho(정병호), Se Dae-Seck(서대석), and Kim Soo-Nam(김수남). *Tongyeong Ogwisaenam-Gut* (통영 오귀새남굿). Seoul: Yeolhwadang(열화당), 1989.
Folklore Research Institute of Won Kwang University(원광대학교 민속학연구소), ed. *The Modern Meaning of Shamanism*(샤마니즘의 현대적 의미). Iri City, Korea: Folklore Research Institute of Won Kwang University, 1973.
Friedlein, Curt. *Geschichte der Philosophie*(서양철학사). Translated by Kang Young-Gye(강영계). Seoul: Seogwangsa(서광사), 1985.
Han Myung-Hee(한명희). *Our Rhythm and Our Culture*(우리가락 우리문화). Seoul: Chosun Ilbo(조선일보), 1994.

———. "A Study on the Aesthetic Features of Korean Traditional Music(한국 음악미의 연구)." PhD diss., Sungkyunkwan University(성균관대학교), 1994.
Hyun, Yong-Jun(현용준), Lee Nam-Duck(이남덕), and Kim Soo-Nam(김수남). *Jejudo Sin-Gut*(제주도신굿). Seoul: Yeolhwadang(열화당), 1989.
Jang, Sa-Hoon(장사훈). *The Introduction to Korean Dance*(한국무용개론). Seoul: Daegwangmunhwasa(대광문화사), 1984.
———. *The Understanding of the Korean Traditional Music*(한국전통음악의 이해). Seoul: Seoul National University Press(서울대학교출판부), 1981.
Jang, Yeon-Hee(장연희). *A Study of Kim Ran Salpuri-Chum as an Intangible Cultural Treasure of Daejeon Metropolitan City*(대전시 지정문화재 김란류 살풀이춤 연구). MA thesis, Mokwon University(목원대학교), 2013.
Joo, Kang-Hyun(주강현). *A Social History of the Gut*(굿의 사회사). Seoul: Woongjin(웅진), 1992.
Kim, In-Hwei(김인회) and Kim Soo-Nam(김수남). *Hwanghaedo Jinogwi-Gut*(황해도 진오귀굿). Seoul: Yelhwadang(열화당), 1993.
Kim, Kyu-Hee(김규희). *The "Hahn" Presented in the Salpuri-Chum*(살풀이춤에 나타난 '恨'의 정서). MA thesis, Wonkwang University(원광대학교), 1997.
Kim, Kyung-Ae(김경애), Kim Chae-Hyun(김채현), and Lee Jong-Ho(이종호). *The Hundred Years of Our Dance*(우리무용 백년). Seoul: Hyunamsa(현암사), 2001.
Kim, Mal-Bok(김말복). *The Understanding of Dance*(무용의 이해). Seoul: Yejeonsa(예전사), 1999.
Kim, Moon-Ae(김문애). *A Study of the Three Salpuri Dancers*(3인의 살풀이춤 탐구). Seoul: Hongkyung(홍경), 1996.
Kim, Soo-Chung(김수청). "A Study of Life, Death, and Ghost in Confucianism(유교의 생사와 귀신문제)." *Sukdangnonchong*(石堂論叢) (Busan, Korea: Sukdang Haksulwon, Dong-A University), 33 (2003):167–182.
Kim, Tae-Gon(김태곤). *The Photographs of Korean Shamanism*(한국무속도록). Seoul: Jipmoondang(집문당), 1982.
Kim, Yong-Shin(김용신). *The Ego Ideal, Ideology, and Hallucination*. Lanham, MD: University Press of America, 1992.
———. *False Image of Leadership*(지도력의 허상). Seoul: Acaone(아카원), 2016.
———. *Ki Dae-Seung, a Theorist of Human Nature, Meets Freud*(성리학자 기대승 프로이트를 만나다). Seoul: Yemunseowon(예문서원), 2002.
———. *A Psychoanalytic Interpretation of Art*(예술의 정신분석학적 해석). Seoul: Nanam(나남), 2008.
———. *Psychology Meets the Korean People*(심리학 한국인을 만나다). Seoul: Sidam(시담), 2010.
———. *Who Am I?: Psychoanalysis for Everyone*(나는 누구인가, 일반인을 위한 정신분석학). Seoul, Salim(살림), 2013.
Ko, Un(고은). *The Sound of My Waves*(내물결의 소리). Seoul: Nanam(나남), 1996.
Koo, Mi-Rae(구미래). *A Symbolic World of the Korean People*(한국인의 상징세계). Seoul: Kyobomunko(교보문고), 1992.
Kook, Min-Ho(국민호). "After-Life of Confucianism Viewed from the Ghost Belief and Ancestral Rites(귀신신앙과 제사를 통해 살펴본 유교의 내세관)." *Society and Theory*(사회와 이론) (Seoul: Association of Korean Social Theory), no. 7 (2005): 93–119.
Lee, Bo-Hyung(이보형). "A Comparative Study of the Generation between Dalgo-Maekki and Gi-Gyeong-Gyeol-Hae: Focused on the Meaning Indicated by the Rhythmic Patterns of Jungjungmori and Jinyang(중중모리 '말고 맺기'와 진양 '기경결해'의 의미 및 생성연구)." *Studies in Korean Music* (Seoul: Korean Musicological Society), no. 39 (2006): 189–235.
Lee, Byung-Ok(이병옥). *History of Korean Dance*(한국무용통사). Seoul: Minsokwon(민속원), 2013.
———. *The Salpuri-Chum: A Study of Its Styles and Lineage*(살풀이춤: 유파와 계통연구). Seoul: Nori(노리), 2008.
Lee, Eun-Joo(이은주). *An Analysis of Salpuri-Chum's Structure*(살풀이춤의 구조분석). PhD diss., Sejong University,1997.

―――. *Han Young Sook's Salpuri-Chum*(한영숙류 살풀이춤). Seoul: Eunhachulpansa(은하출판사), 1992.
―――. *The Thirty Three Dancers*(춤 33인). Seoul: Pureun Media(푸른 메디아), 2007.
Lee, Gyu-Won(이규원) and Chung Bum-Tae(정범태). *The Hundred Korean Traditional Artists*(우리 전통예인 백사람). Seoul: Hyunamsa(현암사), 1995.
Lee, Neung-Hwa(이능화). *A History of Hae-Er-Hwa in the Chosun Dynasty*(조선 해어화역사). Seoul: Dongmunsun(동문선), 1992.
―――. *Study of the Chosun Shamanism*(조선 무속연구). Seoul: Association of Korean Culture and Anthropology(한국문화인류학연구회), 1968
Lee, Sang-Il(이상일). *Gut and Play of the Korean People*(한국인, 굿과 놀이). Seoul: Muneumsa(문음사), 1981.
Lee, Song(이송). "A Study on the Creative Spirit and Historical Significance of Han Seon-Jun's Dance(한성준 춤의 창작정신과 역사적 의의)." *Study Of Korean Dance*(한국무용연구) (Korean Dance Study Association), no. 24 (2006): 155–176.
Lee, Yong-Joo(이용주). "Ghost, a Repressed Desire from Others." *Tradition and the Present* (전통과 현대) (Seoul: Jeontong and Hyundae) 18 (Winter 2001): 34–47.
Lim, Seok-Jae(임석재) and Kim Soo-Nam(김수남). *Wido Tibae-Gut*(위도 띠배굿). Seoul: Yelhwadang(열화당), 1993.
Moon, Il-Ji(문일지). *The Heart to Protect Dance*(춤을 지키는 마음). Seoul: Korean Dance Academy(한국무용아카데미), 1969.
Oh, Hwa-Jin(오화진). *A History of Korean Dance through the study of Dancers*(인물로본 한국무용사). Seoul: Yeronsa(예론사), 1992.
Whang, Ru-Si(황루시) and Kim Soo-Nam(김수남). *Geojedo Byulsin-Gut*(거제도 별신굿). Seoul: Yeolhwadang(열화당), 1993.
Yoo, Dong-Sik(유동식). *The History and Structure of Korean Shamanism*(한국무교의 역사와 구조). Seoul: Yonsei University Press(연세대학교출판부), 1978.
Yoo, In-Hwa(유인화). *I Want to Know the Korean Dance*(한국춤이 알고 싶다). Seoul: East Asia(동아시아), 2014.

ENGLISH PUBLICATIONS

Adorno, Theodore. *The Authoritarian Personality*. New York: Harper, 1952.
Alford, Fred. *Melanie Klein & Critical Social Theory*. New Haven: Yale University Press, 1989.
―――. *Narcissism: Socrates, The Frankfurt School, and Psychoanalytic Theory*. New Haven: Yale University Press, 1988.
Badcock, C. R. *The Psychoanalysis of Culture*. Oxford: Basil Blackwell, 1980.
Bandura, Albert. *Aggression: Social Learning Analysis*. Englewood Cliffs, NJ: Prentice-Hall, 1973.
Benjamin, Jessica. *The Bond of Love*. New York: Pantheon Books, 1988.
Berns, Laurence. "Thomas Hobbes." In *History of Political Philosophy*, edited by Leo Strauss and Joseph Cropsey, 396–420. 3rd ed. Chicago: University of Chicago Press, 1987.
Bion, W. R. *Experiences in Groups and Other Papers*. London: Tavistock, 1961.
Bloodworth, Dennis. *The Chinese Looking Glass*. New York: Dell, 1966.
Bruce, J. Percy, trans. *The Philosophy of Human Nature by Chu Hsi*. London: Probsthain, 1922.
Bunzel, Ruth. *Experiences in Chinese Culture*. Columbia University, Research in Contemporary Culture, 1950. (Mimeo).
Chasseguet-Smirgel, Janine. *The Ego Ideal: A Psychoanalytic Essay on the Malady of the Ideal*. 1st American ed. New York: W.W. Norton, 1985.
―――. "Some Thoughts on the Ego Ideal: A Contribution to the Study of the 'Illness of Ideality.'" *The Psychoanalytic Quarterly* 45 (July 1976), 345–373.
Confucius. *The Analects*. Translated and annotated by Arthur Waley. New York: Vintage Books, 1938.

Bibliography

De Bary, William Theodore, ed. *Sources of Chinese Tradition*. 2 vol. USA: Columbia University Press, 1960.
Desmond, Jane C., ed. *Meaning in Motion: New Cultural Studies of Dance*. Durham: Duke University Press, 1997.
Fodor, Nandor and Frank Gaynor, eds. *Freud: Dictionary of Psychoanalysis*. Westport, Connecticut: Greenwood Press, 1975.
Fordham, Frieda. *An Introduction to Jung's Psychology*. New York: Penguin Books, 1966.
Foster, Susan Leigh, ed. *Corporealities: Dancing Knowledge, Culture and Power*. New York: Routledge, 1996.
Freud, Sigmund. "Beyond the Pleasure Principle." In *1920–1922, Beyond the Pleasure Principle, Group psychology, and Other works*. Vol. 18 of *The Standard Edition of the Complete Psychological Works of Sigmund Freud*. Translated and edited by James Strachey, in collaboration with Anna Freud, assisted by Alix Strachey and Alan Tyson (hereafter cited as *SE*). (London: The Hogarth Press and the Institute of Psycho-Analysis, 1955): 1–64.
———. *Civilization and Its Discontents*. Translated and edited by James Strachey. W.W. Norton, 1961.
———. "The Ego and the Id." In *1923–1925, The Ego and the Id and Other works*. Vol. 19 of *SE*. (1961): 13–68.
———. "Formulations on the Two Principles of Mental Functioning." In *1911–1913, The Case of Schreber, Papers on technique and Other works*. Vol. 12 of *SE*. (1958): 213–26.
———. *The Future of an Illusion*. Translated and edited by James Strachey. New York: W.W. Norton, 1961.
———. *A General Selection from the Works of Sigmund Freud*. New York: Doubleday Anchor Books, 1957.
———. *Group Psychology and the Analysis of the Ego*. Translated and edited by James Strachey. New York: W.W. Norton, 1959.
———. *Introductory Lectures on Psychoanalysis*. Translated and edited by James Strachey. New York: W.W. Norton, 1966.
———. *On Dreams*. Translated and edited by James Strachey. New York: W.W. Norton, 1952.
———. "On Narcissism: An Introduction." In *1914–1916, On the history of the psychoanalytic movement, Papers on metapsychology and Other works*. Vol. 14 of *SE*. (1957): 67–104.
———. *Totem and Taboo*. Translated by James Strachey. New York: W.W. Norton, 1950.
———. "The Unconscious," *SE*, 14:156–216.
Glass, James. *Delusion: Internal Dimensions of Public Life*. Chicago: Chicago University Press, 1985.
Goodman, Nelson. *Languages of Art: An Approach to a Theory of Symbols*. Indianapolis: Bobbs-Merrill, 1968.
Greenberg, Jay R. and Stephen A. Mitchell. *Object Relations in Psychoanalytic Theory*. Cambridge: Harvard University Press, 1983.
Grunberger, B. *Narcissism, Psychoanalytic Essays*. New York: International Universities Press, 1979.
Guntrip, Harry. *Personality Structure and Human Interaction: The Developing Synthesis of Psycho-dynamic Theory*. New York: International Universities Press, 1961.
Hall, Calvin. *A Primer of Freudian Psychology*. New York: World Publishing Company, 1954.
Heidegger, Martin. *Martin Heidegger: Basic Writings*. Edited by David Farrell Krell. New York: Harper & Row, 1977.
Huhm Halla Pai. *Kut: Korean Shamanist Ritual*. Elizabeth, NJ: Hollym International, 1980.
Jung, C. C. *The Undiscovered Self*. Translated by R. F. C. Hall. New York: New American Library, 1958.
Kernberg, Otto. *Internal World and External Reality: Object Relations Theory Applied*. New York: J. Aronson, 1980.
Kim, Yong-Shin. *The Ego Ideal, Ideology, and Hallucination*. Lanham, MD: University Press of America, 1992.
Klein, Melanie. *Contribution to Psychoanalysis*. London: Hogarth Press, 1968.

———. *The Writings of Melanie Klein*. London: Hogarth Press, 1975.
Knafo, Danielle. *Dancing with the Unconscious: The Art of Psychoanalysis and the Psychoanalysis of Art*. New York: Routledge, 2012.
Ko, Un, *The Sound of My Waves: Selected Poems of Ko Un*. Translated by Brother Anthony of Taize and Kim Young-Moo. Ithaca: Cornell University Press, 1993.
Langer, Susanne. *Problems of Art: Ten Philosophical Lectures*. New York: Scribner's, 1957.
Lauen, Gerard. *Sigmund Freud: The Man and His Theories*. New York: Fawcett World Library, 1962.
Le Bon, Gustave. *The Crowd: A Study of the Popular Mind*. United States: Digireads.Com, 2008.
Loewe, Michael. *Chinese Ideas of Life and Death: Faith, Myth, and Reason in the Han Period (202 BC–AD 220)*. Translated by Sung-Kyoo Lee. London: George Allen & Unwin, 1982.
Marcuse, Herbert. *The Aesthetic Dimension*. Boston: Beacon Press, 1978.
———. *Eros and Civilization*. Boston: Beacon Press, 1966.
McDougall, William. *The Group Mind: a sketch of the principles of colletive* [sic] *psychology, with some attempt to apply them to the interpretation of national life and character*. Cambridge: University Press / Ann Arbor, MI: University of Michigan Library, 1920 [reprint].
McNamara, Patrick. *Rites to Become Possessed, Rites to Exorcise "Demons."* Vol. 2 of *Spirit Possession and Exorcism: History, Psychology, and Neurobiology*. Santa Barbara, California: Praeger, 2011.
Mitscherlich, Alexander. *Society without the Father: A Contribution to Social Psychology*. Translated by Eric Mosbacher. New York: Harcourt, Brace & World; London: Tavistock Publications, 1969.
Nietzsche, Friedrich. *Beyond Good and Evil*. Translated by Walter Kaufmann. New York: Vintage Books, 1966.
———. *Will to Power*. Translated by Walter Kaufmann and R. J. Hollingdale. Edited by Walter Kaufmann. New York: Vintage Books, 1968.
Plato. *Great Dialogues of Plato*. Translated by W. H. D. Rouse. New York: A Mentor Book, 1956.
Ramstedt, G. J. *Studies in Korean Etymology*, ed. Pentti Aalto (Helsinki: Suomalais-ugrilainen seura, 1953)
Storr, Anthony. *Jung*. London: Fontana Press, 1973.
Strauss, Leo and Joseph Cropsey, eds. *History of Political Philosophy*. 3rd ed. Chicago: University of Chicago Press, 1987.
Sullivan, Harry S. *The Interpersonal Theory of Psychiatry*. New York: Norton, 1953.
The Douay Bible House. *The Holy Bible*. Translated from the Latin Vulgate. New York: The Douay Bible House, 1953.
Tylor, Edward B. *Primitive Culture: Researches into the Development of Mythology, Philosophy, Religion, Language, Art, and Custom*. New York: G. P. Putnam's Sons, 1920.
Waley, Arthur. *Three Ways of Thought in Ancient China*. New York: Random House, 1956.
Wallace, Anthony F. C. *Culture and Personality*. New York: Random House, 1962.
Weber, Max. *On Charisma and Institution Building*. Chicago: University of Chicago Press, 1968.
Wright, Arthur. *Buddhism in Chinese History*. Stanford: Stanford University Press, 1959.
———, ed. *Studies in Chinese Thoughts*. Chicago: Chicago University Press, 1953.
Wright, Huntington. *What Nietzsche Taught*. New York: B. W. Huebsch, 1917.

Sources of Photographs

Photo 1: *Gopuri Performance*. Courtesy of Lee Eun-Joo (co-author).
Photo 2: *Gilgareum Performance*. Courtesy of Lee Eun-Joo.
Photo 3: *Sinawi Accompaniment*. Courtesy of Lee Gwan-Woong (player of Sinawi music).
Photo 4: *Han Young-Sook's Salpuri-Chum*. Chung Byung-Ho(정병호), *Dances of Korea*(한국춤) (Seoul: Yeolhwadang, 1985), 216.
Photo 5: *Han Young-Sook's Salpuri-Chum*. Chung Byung-Ho, Dances of Korea, 217.
Photo 6: *Han Young-Sook's Salpuri-Chum*. Chung Byung-Ho, Dances of Korea, 218.
Photo 7: *Lee Mae-Bang's Salpuri-Chum*. Chung Byung-Ho, Dances of Korea, 225.
Photo 8: *Lee Mae-Bang's Salpuri-Chum*. Chung Byung-Ho, Dances of Korea, 226.
Photo 9: *Lee Mae-Bang's Salpuri-Chum*. Chung Byung-Ho, Dances of Korea, 227.
Photo 10: *Kim Sook-Ja's Dosalpuri-Chum*. Chung Byung-Ho, Dances of Korea, 220.
Photo 11: *Kim Sook-Ja's Dosalpuri-Chum*. Chung Byung-Ho, Dances of Korea, 222.
Photo 12: *Kim Sook-Ja's Dosalpuri-Chum*. Chung Byung-Ho, Dances of Korea, 223.
Photos 13-14: *Kwon Myung-Hwa's Salpuri-Chum*. Courtesy of Kwon Myung-Hwa.
Photos 15-16: *Choi Sun's Salpuri-Chum*. Courtesy of Choi Sun.
Photos 17-18: *Kim Bok-Ryun's Salpuri-Chum*. Courtesy of Kim Bok-Ryun.

Photos 19-20: *Kim Ran's Salpuri-Chum*. Courtesy of Kim Ran.
Photos 21-26: *Lee Eun-Joo's Salpuri-Chum*. Courtesy of Lee Eun-Joo.

Index

ajaeng, 35
Alford, Fred, 5, 8, 9, 12
An Gyun(安堅), 6, 8
Anpyungdaegun(安平大君), 6
Apollo, art of, 8, 9
art, purpose of, vi, 4–5, 6, 7–8; realism in, 8. *See also* ego ideal and the role of art

baek(魄), 25–26, 44
baek-eui-min-jok(白衣民族), 44
ballet, western, 44, 60, 62, 76, 77, 78
bara, 35
barksoo(박수), 30, 55
Buddhism, 18, 22, 25, 65
buk(북), 35, 64
Bumingwan(府民館), 44, 47n13, 49, 67
Bupgomu(法鼓舞), 65

catharsis, 9, 14, 20, 34, 39, 40–41, 62, 77, 78, 80
changwoo(倡優), 40
Chasseguet-Smirgel, Janine, 3, 4
Cheoyong-Mu(處容舞), 63, 66, 69
Choi Nam-Sun(崔南善), 31
Choi Sun(崔仙), 56, 57, 70
Cho Ji-Hoon(趙芝薰), 13
chosangsin(祖上神), 26
Chosun(朝鮮) dynasty, 6, 12, 40, 42, 43, 58, 63, 65, 66–67
chum(춤), 14
Chun Yi-Du(千二斗), 12

Chung Gyung-Pa, 58
Chung Sun(鄭歚), 8
collective unconscious, vi, 14, 15, 17, 19, 20
Confucius, 39
Confucianism, 9, 18, 19, 25, 26, 39, 65, 66
constancy principle, 7, 8, 77
Courbet, Gustave, 8

daegeum(대금), 35, 65
dajeongga(多情歌), 21
dalgo(달고), 46
dangol(당골), 31
Dionysus, art of, 9
Dodang(都堂)-Gut, 52, 53, 70
dongcho(童草), 57
Dongcho Salpuri-Chum, 57
dosalpuri(도살푸리), 53, 60
Dosalpuri-Chum, 52
durumagi(두루마기), 57

ego, 2, 3, 15
ego ideal, vi, vii, 1, 2–4, 10n11, 13, 15, 21, 32, 36, 74; and the role of art, 4, 5, 6, 9
Eros, 5, 16, 17
erotization, 7
evil spirit, v, 11, 25, 26, 27, 28, 31–32, 34, 45, 52, 53, 66, 69, 74, 75, 77

Freud, Sigmund, 2, 3, 7, 8, 15–17, 26, 27, 77

gayakum(伽倻琴), 35
Geomgi-Mu, 63
Geom-Mu(劍舞), 44
geomungo(거문고), 35
gi (起), 41, 42, 63; in rhythm structure, 46
gilgareum(길가름), 32
gisang(妓生), 41–43, 44, 56, 63–64
Gisang-Chum, 39, 43, 56
Goodman, Nelson, 4
gopuri(고풀이), 32, 56
Greenberg, Jay R., 2
gueum(口音), 35, 58
Guntrip, Harry, 16
gut(굿), v, vi, 28, 29, 30, 31–32, 33, 40, 42, 52, 56, 74
gwangdae(廣大), 39, 40–41, 42, 43, 44
Gwangdae-Chum, 39
gwangi(官妓), 42, 43
gwisin(鬼神), 26
gwonbeon(券番), 43, 50, 55, 56
gyemyunjo(界面調), 36–37, 51, 56
gyeol(結), 46
gyeong(輕), 46
Gyeonggi(京畿), 36, 50, 52, 58, 67, 70
gyobang(敎坊), 42
Gyobangcheong(敎坊廳), 42, 64

hae(解), 41, 46
hae-er-hwa(解語花), 41
haegeum(해금), 35, 64, 65
hahn(한), vii, 11–13, 14, 19, 20, 28, 29, 34, 36, 41, 42, 51, 59, 74–75, 76; in the souls of the dead, 28, 31–32, 33, 45, 59. *See also* evil spirit
Hall, Calvin, 2–3
hallucination, 3, 21, 28, 34, 36, 76
Hanlyang-Mu(閑良舞), 44
Han Myung-Hee, 33
hansam(汗衫), 64, 68
hansoom(한숨), 34
Han Sung-Jun(韓成俊), 43, 47n13, 49, 51, 52, 61, 65, 67, 69, 75
Han Young-Sook(韓英淑), 45, 49, 51, 52, 60, 61–62, 65, 67, 68, 69–70, 71, 79
Hark-Mu(鶴舞), 44, 66, 67
Hark-Yeonhwadae-Hapsul-Mu(鶴蓮花臺合設舞), 63, 66, 67, 69
Heidegger, Martin, 6

heung(흥), vii, 19, 36, 40–41, 42, 43, 57, 60, 62, 75, 77
hon(魂), 25–26, 26
Honam(湖南), 36, 51, 55, 56, 58, 59
Honam Salpuri-Chum, 57
hwa-byung(화병), 12
hwamunsuk(花紋席), 57
Hwarang-Jedo(花郎制度), 41
Hwasung Jaeincheong, 58
Hwasung Jaeincheong Salpuri-Chum, 58
hyangga(鄉歌), 35
Hyekyungkunghongsi(惠慶宮洪氏), 12

illusion, 3
immanence, vii, 8, 9
Institute of Chosun Music and Dance, 44, 49
interpersonal psychoanalysis, 16, 17
introjection, 17, 18, 25

jaein(才人), 40
Jaeincheong(才人廳), 40, 58
jangku(장구), 35, 58, 64, 65
jeon(轉), 32, 46
jeong(情), 13, 20, 21–22, 74, 78
jeongak(正樂), 42
jer, 64
jijeon, 32
jing(징), 35, 58
Jinju Geom-Mu(晉州劍舞), 63, 64, 69
jokduri(족두리), 64
jung-joong-dong(靜中動), 78, 79
jupsin(接神), 31
Jupsin-Gut, 30

Kang Sun-Young(姜善泳), 68
Karl-Chum(칼춤), 63
ki(氣), 39
Kim Bok-Ryun(金福蓮), 58, 59, 60, 70
Kim Hong-Do(金弘道), 8
Kim Ran(金蘭), 59, 60, 70
Kim Sook-Ja(金淑子), 45, 52, 53, 58–59, 60, 69–70
Kim So-Wol(金素月), 12
Kim Yong-Shin(金容新), 21
Klein, Melanie, 17, 21
Knafo, Danielle, 4
Kochosun(古朝鮮), kingdom of, 18
Koguryeo(高句麗), kingdom of, 14, 18, 67

Korean traditional music, characteristics of, 13, 33–34, 36, 44, 46, 55, 68; compared to western music, 33, 34
Koryeo-Yeoak(高麗女樂), 41
Ko Un(高銀), 28
kutu, 29
kwaeja(쾌자), 51, 57, 64
kwangwari(꽹과리), 58

Langer, Susanne, 4
Le Bon, Gustave, 15
Lee Eun-Joo(李銀珠), 33, 49, 55, 60, 61, 70
Lee Jo-Nyun(李兆年), 21
Lee Mae-Bang(李梅芳), 45, 50, 52, 56, 57, 69–70, 79
li(理), 39

maetgo(맺고), 46
Manchuria, 18
Marcuse, Herbert, 5, 7
McDougall, William, 15
McNamara, Patrick, 26
milgo(밀고), 46
Mitchell, Stephen A., 2
Mitscherlich, Alexander, 3
Mongyoodowondo(夢遊桃源圖), 6
mudang(巫堂), 30, 55
myungdang(明堂), 27, 33, 73

nambawoo(남바우), 51
narcissism, 2, 3, 8, 9, 76–77, 78, 80
neo-Freudian school, 16
Nietzsche, Friedrich, 2, 8, 9
Nongae(論介), 63

object relation theory, 2, 15, 17, 20, 22
oedipal phase, 3
Oedipus complex, 3, 26
ohaeng(五行), 33, 66
oryun(五倫), 18, 23n27

pansori(판소리), 13
piri(피리), 35, 64, 65
Plato, 6, 39
pleasure principle, 3–4
polymorphous sexuality, 7
poong-soo(風水), 27
pregenital, 7

primary narcissism, 3, 8, 9
projection, 17, 18, 25, 75
psychosexual development, 8
pulgo(풀고), 46
puri(풀이), 11, 14, 29, 32

qut, 29
qutug, 29

Ramstedt, G. J., 29
reality principle, 3, 3–4, 16

Sado(思悼), 12
sal(煞), 11, 14, 28, 29
salpuri(살풀이), 11, 14, 28, 31, 34, 53, 75, 76, 77
Salpuri-Chum(살풀이춤), v, vii, 14, 15, 19, 29, 31, 33, 43–45, 50, 63, 69, 75; aesthetic elements, 77–78, 79–80; artistic forms, 75–77; basic structure of, 45; current situation of, 70–71; differences from other Korean traditional dances, 68–69; philosophical principles, 73–74, 75; rhythm structure of, 45–46
Salpuri-Chum, main styles: Han Young-Sook style, 49–50, 70, 71; Kim Sook-Ja style, 52–53, 70; Lee Mae-Bang style, 51, 70
Salpuri-Chum, other styles: Choi Sun style, 57–58, 70; Kim Bok-Ryun style, 58–59, 70; Kim Ran style, 60, 70; Kwon Myung-Hwa style, 56, 70; Lee Eun-Joo style, 61–62, 70
Salpuri-Gut(살풀이굿), 31, 32, 33, 34, 45, 52, 74
samgang(三綱), 18, 23n27
samhyunyookgak(三絃六角), 35, 58, 59, 62
sanoega(詞腦歌), 35
Sejong(世宗), 6, 66
Sejong University, 49, 60, 61
self-preservation, 1–2, 7, 8, 15, 77
self-realization, 1, 2
self-satisfaction, 2, 14
seung(承), 46
Seungjeon-Mu(勝戰舞), 63, 64, 69
Seung-Mu(僧舞), 44, 65, 68, 69

shaman, v, 14, 29–30, 31–32, 34, 35, 36, 40, 41, 52, 59, 67–68
shamanism, 28–29, 30, 35
Shin Yoon-Bok(申潤福), 8
Silla(新羅), kingdom of, 6, 35, 41, 63, 66
simbang(심방), 35
simbang-gok(심방곡), 35
sinak(神樂), 35
sinawi(시나위), 35
sinawi rhythm, v, 33, 34, 35–36, 45, 50, 51, 53, 68, 75–76, 80; development of, 40, 42, 43, 44, 55, 56, 57–58, 62, 70. *See also* Korean traditional music
sinbang(神房), 35
sinbaram(신바람), 36
sin-byung(神病), 30, 55, 58
sindang(神堂), 30, 31
sinlyung(神靈), 26
Soogun-Chum(수건춤), 43
sublimation, vii, 7, 8, 9, 14, 62, 65, 76, 78, 80
Sullivan, Harry Stack, 16, 17

Sunglidaejeon(性理大全), 25
superego, 2–3, 3–4, 10n11

taeguk(太極), 59
Taepyung-Mu(太平舞), 44, 63, 67, 68, 69
thanatos, 16, 17
transcendence, 5, 8
Trotter, Wilfred, 15

Wang San-Ak(王山岳), 67
Weber, Max, 31
Westermarck, Edvard, 27
wish model, 2
Wonhwa-Jedo(源花制度), 41

yang(陽), 33, 37n9, 59
Yimjinwaeran(壬辰倭亂), 63, 64
yin(陰), 33, 37n9, 59
Yi Sun-Sin(李舜臣), 64
Yoo Chi-Hwan(柳致環), 32
yookche(肉體), 25
Youngjo(英祖), 12

About the Authors

LEE EUN-JOO (李銀珠; PEN NAME, NOEUL: 露乙)

Lee Eun-Joo was born in Korea. She started learning dance in elementary school. During middle school, she received first prize in the National Student Dance Competition. She received her BA and MA degrees in dance from Sejong University, where she became a student of famous Korean traditional dancer, Han Young-Sook, who greatly contributed the development of Salpuri-Chum. After obtaining her master's, Lee went to Germany where she studied philosophy at Joann Wolfgang Goethe University-Frankfurt.

After returning to Seoul, she received the presidential prize in the Third National Dance Competition. She obtained her PhD in physical education, with a major in dance, from Sejong University. Her dissertation was titled "An Analysis of Salpuri-Chum's Structure." In order to teach and propagate Salpuri-Chum, Lee established the Association for the Preservation of Han Yong-Sook Salpuri-Chum. And in 2015, she was named a living human cultural treasure of Seoul Special City (No. 46) in the field of Salpuri-Chum.

Lee authored *Han Young-Sook's Salpuri-Chum*(한영숙 살풀이춤), *The Thirty Three Dancers*(춤 33인), and many articles related to Salpuri-Chum. In addition, she has held more than 50 personal dance performances in Korea, and has participated in the various dance festivals in many countries. She now holds the positions of professor of Incheon National University, Chairwoman of the Association for Preservation of Han Yong-Sook Salpuri-Chum, and vice chairwoman of the Korea Dance Association.

KIM YONG-SHIN (金容新; PEN NAME, YIDANG: 怡堂)

Kim Yong-Shin was born in Korea. After receiving his BA in political science and two MA degrees (one in political science, and the other in history) in Korea, he went to the United States, where he received another MA in political science from George Washington University, and a PhD in political philosophy from the University of Maryland at College Park. His major for the PhD was psychoanalytic social and political theory. His dissertation was "The Ego Ideal, Ideology, and Hallucination," which was published by University Press of America in 1992.

Apart from his study of psychoanalytic theory, Kim has studied Oriental calligraphy since he was five years old. He has held five personal exhibitions (four in Seoul and one in Chicago), and has published three books introducing his own calligraphic works. Recently, he created a new approach to Oriental calligraphy. He calls it "Vital Symbolism," which emphasizes the vitality of each stroke and the symbolic representation of the letters.

He has authored many books related to Oriental calligraphy, as well as on psychoanalytic social and political theory. Among them, *Who Am I?: Psychoanalysis for Everyone* (나는 누구인가?: 일반인을 위한 정신분석학), *Aesthetics of Oriental Calligraphy*(서의 미학), *Psychology meets the Korean People* (심리학 한국인을 만나다), and *A Psychoanalytic Interpretation of Art*(예술의 정신분석학적 해석), are partly related to the subject of this book. Kim currently is chair professor of Korea International Culture University of Graduate, and also chairman of the Korea Independent Workers Association.

www.ingramcontent.com/pod-product-compliance
Lightning Source LLC
Chambersburg PA
CBHW051103230426
43667CB00013B/2423